Climbing!
From
Toproping
to Sport

Nate Fitch and
Ron Funderburke

FALCONGUIDES

GUILFORD, CONNECTICUT
HELENA, MONTANA

FALCONGUIDES®

An imprint of Rowman & Littlefield

Falcon, FalconGuides, Make Adventure Your Story, and How to Climb are registered trademarks of Rowman & Littlefield.

Distributed by NATIONAL BOOK NETWORK

Copyright © 2016 by Rowman & Littlefield

British Library Cataloguing in Publication Information available

Library of Congress Cataloging-in-Publication Data

Names: Fitch, Nate. | Funderburke, Ron.
Title: Climbing : from Toproping to sport / Nate Fitch and Ron Funderburke.
Description: Guilford, Connecticut : FalconGuides, [2016] | "Distributed by NATIONAL BOOK NETWORK"—T.p. verso.
Identifiers: LCCN 2016006027| ISBN 9781493016396 (paperback) | ISBN 9781493025268 (eBook)
Subjects: LCSH: Rock climbing—Handbooks, manuals, etc.
Classification: LCC GV200.2 .F547 2016 | DDC 796.522/3—dc23
LC record available at http://lccn.loc.gov/2016006027

∞™ The paper used in this publication meets the minimum requirements of American National Standard for Information Sciences—Permanence of Paper for Printed Library Materials, ANSI/NISO Z39.48-1992.

Contents

Introduction: What Is Sport Climbing?

Every climber will eventually have an opinion about sport climbing. For some, *sport climbing* is an oxymoron; their bumper stickers deride, "Sport climbing is neither!" At the same time, many climbers —the majority of climbers, in fact—regard outdoor sport climbing as the most approximate version of the lead climbing they enjoy indoors. Their earliest outdoor climbing experiences seek the familiar, the accessible, and the secure, and they probably could care less what other people think of how they choose to climb. Most impressively, climbing's most elite free climbers all regard sport climbing as one of the predominant proving grounds of human potential. Indisputably, whether sport climbing is derided, or familiar, or avant-garde, it is part of American climbing, and it is here to stay.

What part of American climbing does sport climbing occupy? Is classifying it really as contentious as it seems? Does it have to be? Perhaps the contentiousness of the category is the most distinctively American thing about American sport climbing. Regardless, we find sport climbing fascinating, nuanced, and challenging. It is not the only way to climb, but it's an enjoyable way.

One of the challenges we faced in writing this book is that all populations of American climbers, regardless of their native climbing disciplines, do not enjoy a consensus about what sport climbing actually is. We all seem to know what we mean when we refer to sport climbing, but the actual discipline, genre, or style of climbing that constitutes sport climbing remains unstated or assumed. What do we mean when we refer to sport climbing? What is a sport climb and how is it different from any other traditional lead climb? What exactly are we trying to prepare readers to do? Where are we trying to prepare them to go? This undefined, inexact, and putative characteristic of sport climbing is treacherous territory, as we discovered in writing this book.

These questions cannot remain unanswered, because an accurate perception of sport climbing must precede any body of instruction on how to do it. It would certainly be easier to speak nebulously about sport climbing, to lean on the general/approximate understanding of the reader, as most texts on the subject tend to do. But, at some point, we have to learn to talk about sport climbing in a way that positions it historically and culturally. We have to define it. We need to say what it is, what it is not, and why that makes sense. If we do not, there is no way to know what we are even trying to do out there, much less how to do it. Let's try to find some common ground about what sport climbing means, what makes it fun, and why sport climbing is one of the ways climbers have learned to play on the rock.

Free Climbing, Lead Climbing, and Style

In *Advanced Rockcraft*, Royal Robbins posed a question that should remain with all climbers to this day. In fact, the question is more relevant now than it ever has been. He wrote, "Why lead? The mystique of being first on the rope has a romantic aura, but little necessary relation to the joy of climbing rock."

If a climber is motivated purely by "the joy of climbing rock," as Robbins observed, then his logic is inescapable. There is no need to ever lead. Toproping and most bouldering present enough variety, venues, and challenges to sate the most voracious climbers for their lifetimes. Many climbers find this truism to be completely satisfactory, and all the adventure they are ever tempted to tackle can be found among the world's inexhaustible supply of boulders, topropes, and climbing gyms.

Sport climbing is different; it is not solely about the joy of climbing rock. Sport climbing involves leading, and it is therefore more akin to the mountaineering, traditional lead climbing (aka trad climbing), and free soloing pursuits that preceded it. If sport climbing were purely about "the joy of climbing rock," then one would have to wonder how absurdly it goes about doing so. Today, we might imagine Robbins asking, "Why sport climb when you can just go toproping or bouldering?"

The answer may be familiar to many readers. Sport climbing does something that enhances "the joy of climbing rock." It is sweetened by parcels of adventure. Its pleasures are heightened by measures of risk, and its novelty is validated by the history and culture of climbing. We think Robbins might agree, as long as we don't destroy the cliff in the process.

Toproping and bouldering are worthwhile pursuits, and they always will be. But a lead climb gives a climber the smallest taste of what it was like for the pioneers of climbing to launch into the unknown. Success is not always assured, and there is a chance that the lead climber will not be able to reach the top. That small parcel of adventure makes sport climbing more alluring than toproping. What's more, the impending risk of a lead fall gives a climber the smallest taste of the risks that mountaineers and traditional lead climbers negotiate. The risk must be managed, but the management is not distracting or debilitating in sport climbing. If done correctly, it can be more casual, more enjoyable, and just scary enough to make it more interesting than toproping or bouldering.

How Did Sport Climbing Originate?

Sport climbing was born for two reasons. First, many of the world's cliffs and crags do not naturally lend themselves to the ground-up development style that "modern" climbers in the 1950s and 1960s forged. In Southern France, for example, the waves of blue limestone were often too friable, or devoid of natural weaknesses, to be protected in the manner that was common in Yosemite Valley. Instead, climbers "prepared" the cliff for lead climbing. They rappelled in from above, placed bolts at increments to protect a lead climber from ground and ledge fall, and installed a permanent anchor for all future climbers to enjoy. Many cliffs were too tall or too steep to be toproped, so these preparatory tactics were (and are) appropriate.

Second, it is difficult to push the limits of one's physical potential, to explore the boundaries of free climbing, when one is grappling with risks that can be managed only through flawless movement. While many cliffs, many climbs, and many cultures prioritize the confluence of risk and movement, the coincidence of cutting-edge free climbing difficulty with do-the-move-or-die risk management is rare. It certainly isn't popular.

So, sport climbing is an understandable answer to this conundrum. Either the cliff didn't lend itself to traditional development or the climbers wanted to take a bit of the edge off the "sharp end" in order to push the boundaries of free climbing. In both contexts, climbers "prepare" the cliff for lead climbing by clearing debris and loose rock, installing anchors and protection bolts, and establishing a certain "line" that follows those preparatory gestures. The ability to "prepare" the cliff has evolved. This evolution has helped the growth of sport climbing. Hand drilling is slow and difficult. Although still practiced, power drills came along in the 80's and made drilling easier, quicker, and of higher quality. Sport climbing protection evolved as well. Modern technology in bolts (described in chapter 3) was another central part of sport climbing's growth.

Subsequently, the lead climber does not have to rise to the challenge of establishing the route. That is a process more akin to traditional lead climbing or civil engineering. Instead, a lead climber simply tries to meet the challenge of leading a route in the best style he/she can manage. Style is a big part of the game. To lead a climb without resting on the rope, without falling, in a calm, assured, and precise manner, imparts the most sublime feeling of mastery. Sport climbers are willing to suffer and labor mightily in order to feel that kind of perfection.

Is Sport Climbing Safe?

On the surface, sport climbing can seem pretty simple. This is not the case. Just read the reports in *Accidents in North American Mountaineering*, the definitive source for

A sport climber in action. This climb could only be protected with sport climbing tactics like bolts.

all forms of climbing accidents; many occur around single pitch/sport climbing sites. The importance of doing your homework (this text and others) and working with a truly skilled and experienced mentor or AMGA climbing professional cannot be overstated. It can be difficult to assess a mentor, and we cannot begin to count all the examples of low-quality mentorship we have witnessed and misinformation/poor practices being passed on to unknowing climbers. Of course, the dissemination of misinformation is further complicated by a misunderstanding of what climbers are being mentored to do, and the unspoken boundaries between sport climbing and trad climbing only compound the problem. Now, more so than ever, a text about sport climbing must answer the question: What is a sport climb?

What Is a Sport Climb?

The origins of sport climbing overlapped and mingled so frequently with traditional lead climbing and route development that the resulting legacy can be difficult to quantify or describe. Suffice it to say, many of the climbs that are often noted as sport climbs have severe and dangerous consequences throughout the lead. So, they feel more like traditional ground-up adventures with traditional ground-up risks. There is a tendency to define climbs as trad, mixed, or sport, and what that actually means can be confusing.

The instruction detailed in this text is predicated on the following definition of a sport climb: A climb is a sport climb if

- The climb deemphasizes risk, adventure, and technical prowess in order to emphasize free climbing difficulty.

- The climb has permanent bolts (the type may vary), in optimal condition, that are placed frequently enough to protect a climber from ground or ledge fall for the entire length of a lead.

- The climb has an obvious and permanent two-bolt anchor at the end of the route that can be cleaned by lowering through permanent rings, quick/rapid links, or carabiners.

- The climb has been largely cleared of conspicuous debris and rockfall hazards.

- The climb is not in a remote or alpine setting.

- The climb does not require intermediate belays to complete. It is a single pitch where length is half a rope length or less.

Since our definition of a sport climb is so rigorous,

many of the climbs that have been historically catego-
rized as sport will have to be reconsidered. Here are a
few examples of the kinds of climbs that are generally
regarded as sport climbs but perhaps deserve to be
recategorized.

Dangerous Climbs

Any number of factors can make a climb dangerous,
so another way of describing a dangerous climb is
one where risk management concerns overshadow
movement. Consider a climb like Bonemaster Gear
Fling 5.11d, located prominently beside the Hon-
eymooner's Ladder, at the Endless Wall of the New
River Gorge in West Virginia. While it is certainly
an enjoyable climb, Bonemaster has won a fearsome
reputation for the emotional trial that an aspiring
lead climber will endure. With difficult moves off the
ground, the initial groundfall risks can be ameliorated
with a stick clip, but the moves above the first bolt
again summon a precise performance. The slightest
miscalculation in sequence, a broken hold, or slippery
conditions will result in groundfall from as high as 25
feet. Unexpected lead falls of this distance combined
with ground impact can and will result in injury, no
matter how quickly or responsively a belayer performs
his/her duty. Once the third bolt is clipped, the leader
enjoys engaging face climbing, with manageable falls,
for the remainder of the pitch.

Relocation of the bolts on Bonemaster could
potentially solve all of these risks, such that a leader
is never in danger of groundfall for the length of the
pitch. But in the meantime, launching into Bonemaster, with an assumption that risk management
concerns will not overshadow the moves on the pitch,

would be unwise. This text will ask the reader to agree that Bonemaster, and the risky climbs like it, are not sport climbs.

Mixed Climbs or "Sporty" Climbs

Many climbs developed alongside traditional lines of weakness were established in ground-up style, and bolts were used to protect sequences of a pitch that were otherwise unprotectable. Before micro-camming devices and other removable protection tools, bolts might have been used more frequently. Nevertheless, climbers who seek to repeat a climb that was established in this style should equip themselves with the same tools, techniques, and judgment that the first ascent used to establish the pitch. In other words, repeating these leads requires a traditional lead climbing skill set, a rack of removable protection, and a certain appetite for adventure. Similarly, a consistently sized crack system might be protected with the same size camming unit from the bottom to the top, but learning to use that unit, however consistently it is applied, is a fundamentally different skill set than the one we will emphasize in this text.

Consider a climb like Waste Not Want Not 5.12, at the North Face of Looking Glass Rock in North Carolina. Because the climb's 80-foot length is punctuated by three bolts and a fixed piton, it is often courted by sport climbers. However, if a climber flirts with Waste Not with mere quickdraws, not only is there the potential for 30- to 40-foot falls off the crux, but also a head-splitting groundfall will invariably result from an unsuccessful attempt to clip the first bolt or the fixed piton that follows. An appropriately prepared lead climber will need small cams to

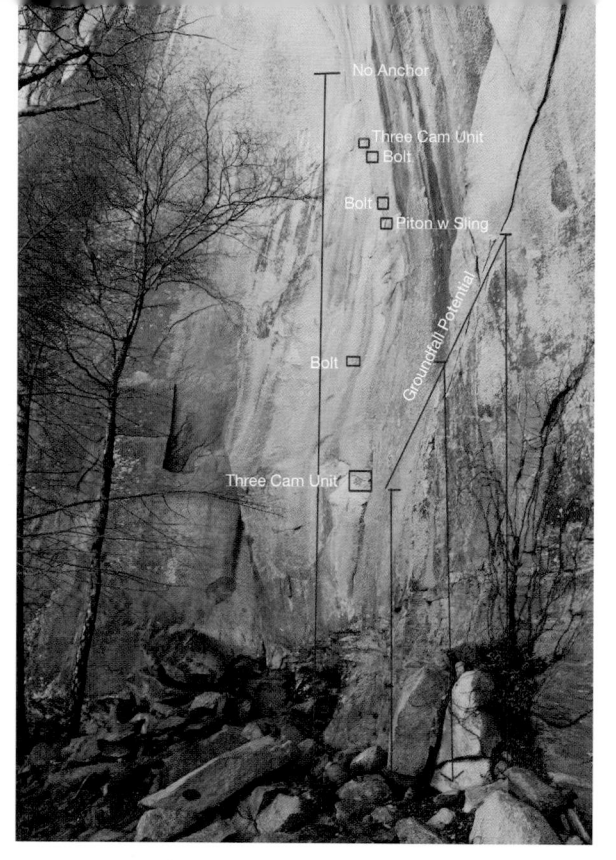

Labels on image:
No Anchor
Three Cam Unit
Bolt
Bolt
Piton w Sling
Groundfall Potential
Bolt
Three Cam Unit

Waste Not Want Not is 5.12 and 80 feet long. As one can see, it clearly does not meet our definition of a sport climb. It's a traditional lead climb because risk management is a higher priority than movement throughout the lead.

protect to the top and the bottom of Waste Not, adequate rope management to reduce rope drag for the tenuous final moves, knowledge of piton-craft and an ability to evaluate that point of the lead, and a strong emotional commitment to strenuous placements and huge fall potential. Waste Not Want Not is a great climb, but a leader will need more than quickdraws to lead it comfortably.

Climbs with Funky Anchors

Many sport climbers cue up for bolt-protected leads that might otherwise fit our definition of a sport climb, but when the leader arrives at the top of the pitch, he/she is often faced with an unclear anchor. So, with little knowledge of the nuanced tasks involved in evaluating, building, or cleaning anchors, the leader is forced to innovate a solution to the problem, rather than focus on climbing.

Consider a climb like Bear Hunt 5.7, located at the Flakeview Area of Rumbling Bald, North

Bear Hunt is a great climb, but its anchor can be difficult to use and evaluate.

Carolina. The climbing is adequately protected, but the lead climber discovers a clump of pine trees at the top of the pitch, with shallow roots, and an heirloom nest of slings, ropes, quick links, or carabiners, contributed by generations of climbers and designated as the anchor. In truth, it is almost always a viable anchor, but confirming that requires careful inspection, an understanding of anchoring principles, and perhaps an occasional offering to the anchor gods when the tattered slings and ropes require replacement. In any of those circumstances, climbers may be dismayed to learn that a modest rack of quickdraws will not suffice.

New Climbs with Lots of Loose Rock

When new climbing areas are discovered, considerable time and effort are placed into cleaning and preparing the rock for travel. But, occasionally, the development of an area is incomplete when the designation of "sport climbing" is given. Or loose rock is intentionally left on the cliff to dissuade sport climbing tactics. Either way, a lead climber who cannot help but rain debris and destruction upon the heads of his/her belayer, onlookers, or other climbers clearly is taking risks that are distracting and hold consequence.

Consider a climbing area like Rocky Face Park, in Alexander County, North Carolina. The climbing at Rocky Face was conjured from an old quarry, and the traumatized blasted rock strata required thorough grooming, testing, and inspection before development could happen in earnest. While much of Rocky Face has been nicely manicured, other climbs are still woefully unstable. It would be imprudent to climb Rocky Face without a helmet. It would be imprudent to even watch climbers there without a helmet. Yet the sport climbing designation undermines these intrinsic hazards.

Sport Climbing Culture, Style, and Terms

Beta: Information about the climb that climbers share with one another. This term originates from Betamax, a short-lived videotape format/player. Early sport climbers would use Betamax videos of themselves and others to analyze the movement in an effort to gain information that would be beneficial during the climb.

Crux: The hardest single move or moves of the climb

Flash: To lead a climb without any falls with some knowledge, but no previous attempts

Hangdog: To take multiple falls and hang in between them

LNT: Leave No Trace. A best practice for all climbers. See www.lnt.org for more info!

Onsight: To lead a climb without any falls, without any prior knowledge

Pinkpoint: To lead a climb without any falls with some knowledge, some previous attempts, and the quickdraws already in place

Redpoint: To lead a climb without any falls with some knowledge and some previous attempts

Red Tag/Project: A red tag hanging from the first bolt of a climb indicates a new project in progress—stay off!

Rope Gun: A person who can shoot up climbs and set them up for others to enjoy

Whip/Whipper: A leader fall

Rumney, New Hampshire, a favorite sport climbing area.

CHAPTER 1

Toproping Review and Sport Climbing Best Practices

What common skills and best practices from toproping do you need to become a sport climber? What skills and best practices are unique to sport climbing? What skills and best practices are needed to be fully prepared for a day of sport climbing? The answers to these questions are not always simple or clear.

As we mentioned in the introduction, sport climbing is a more advanced skill set than toproping. So, an ideal progression as an outdoor rock climber begins with those rudimentary skills learned in a toproping

A kiosk and various signs from climbing areas—please read and follow!

environment. The transitions disclosed in this text depend largely on a prerequisite skill set honed in a toprope setting, at a climbing gym, or with a mentor. It is a common theme in rock climbing, and in human nature, to dive straight into the most ambitious and exhilarating aspects of an activity. However, in rock climbing this kind of overanxiousness and ambition can be dangerous. More practically, circumventing a firm grasp of foundational skills just delays the eventual outcome one seeks to achieve. Even if one arrives at some arbitrary goalpost earlier than others, what benefit is derived? What risks are accrued? This text will strongly assert that the benefits are negligible and the risks are plentiful. Before attempting to learn to sport climb, learn to toprope.

Briefly we will review the toproping skills relevant to sport climbing. Before attempting to learn to sport climb, one should have the following:

- A working knowledge of common climbing equipment: helmet, harness, shoes, belay hardware (plate/aperture/tube devices and ABDs), locking and nonlocking carabiners, ropes, cords, and runners. Use, care for, and retire per the manufacturer's specifications.

- A working knowledge of common climbing knots and hitches: the figure 8 follow through, the figure 8 on a bight, the autoblock friction hitch, the clove hitch, the BHK.

- A working knowledge of a toprope belay system that allows for a variety of crag types, and an understanding of the fundamental principles of belay, setup and double checks, belaying and lowering, the use of an ABD and an aperture/plate/tube device, arresting a fall, and communication.

- An ability to climb 5th class terrain on a variety of terrain features, including slabs, cracks, overhangs, and face climbs. Additionally, one should strive to climb at the 5.7–5.8 level at a minimum. Sport climbs at these levels are hard to come by, and easier sport climbs are even more difficult to find.

- An understanding of Leave No Trace principles and how they apply to an outdoor climbing venue.

- An understanding and utilization of best practices for general climbing applications and risk management, backups and double checks, closing the system, site use, belaying, rappelling, and anchoring.

- **Personal responsibility** in the above areas, acceptable use of climbing resources, and emergency preparedness.

If some of these prerequisite skills are rusty or unproven, the previous texts in this series can be of great use, especially *Climbing: Gym to Rock, Climbing:*

Do you know these knots, hitches, and bends?

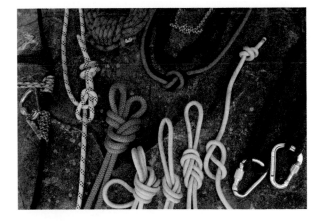

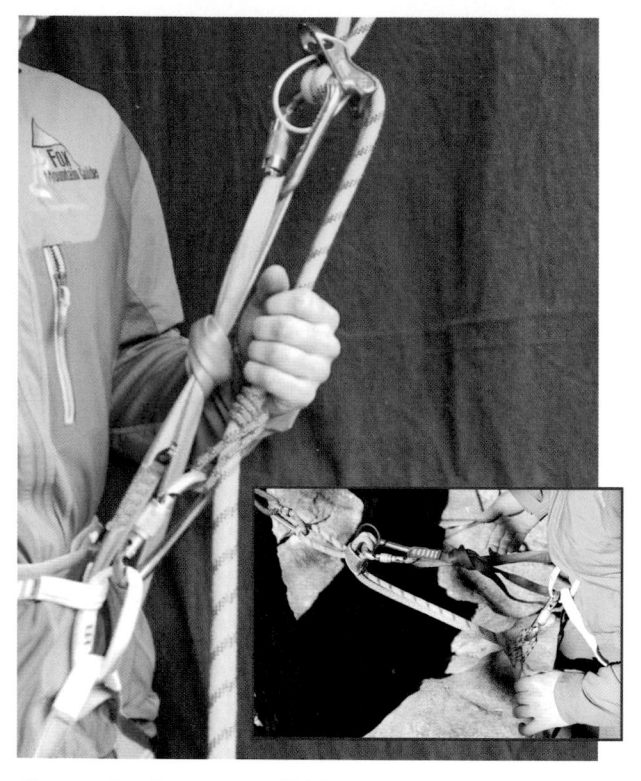

Can you back up a rappel? The extended rappel device and autoblock backup is an effective method.

Protection, and *Climbing: Knots*. All the techniques mentioned in this text build on and add to those mentioned in previous texts. We hope that this text can accompany appropriate practice/instruction/mentorship so that the reader can become a sport climbing leader. Before attempting to learn to sport climb, one will also need the following UIAA endorsed equipment that is within its working lifespan, or at least have access to these items throughout an outing:

Can you build this NERDSS toprope anchor and manage risk while doing so?

- UIAA-approved climbing helmet
- UIAA-approved climbing harness
- 60–70m dynamic rope
- At least 2 locking pear-shaped or HMS locking carabiners per person (4 total)
- At least 10–15 quickdraws
- Anchor materials (48-inch nylon sling or 16–18 feet of 7mm nylon cordellette)
- Attachment materials (standard nylon sling or daisy link)
- Tube/aperture/plate belay device (ATC, Reverso, or other)
- ABD (GriGri or other)

- Accessory cord loop for friction hitches
- Chalk
- Sport climbing specific—see later chapters

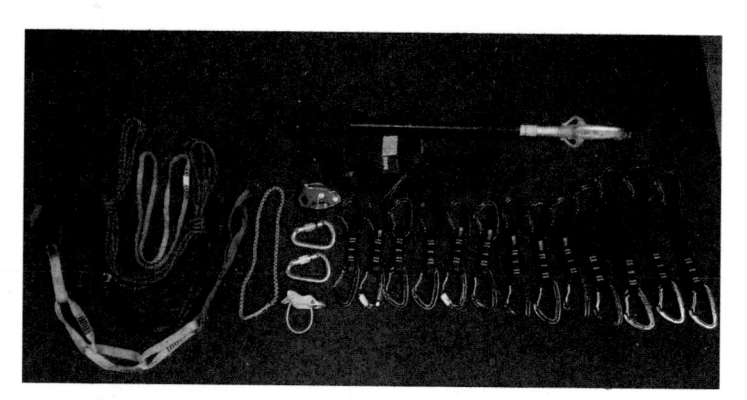

Equipment—aside from helmet, harness, and rope— needed for a day of sport climbing.

Chapter 2 will further investigate equipment and preparation.

These prerequisites are just a start. If you are not there yet, reading this text can still be an edifying experience, but it will probably not be practically oriented. For practice, you will need an effective safety net to help you fill in the gaps, so it is advisable to seek additional instruction and mentorship to accompany this book.

Savvy sport climbers in action. They employ best practices and possess a well-rounded skill set.

The following sport climbing flowchart will serve as an overview of the process of sport climbing and represents the skill set an experienced sport climbing leader possesses. The skills and decision-making process on the chart will be covered in the chapters that follow.

Pre-outing: Research • Recruit/join climbing team • Prepare equipment and pack • Learn about land management and specific LNT concerns.

▼

Pre-climb: Find the climb • Establish a locker room • Get dressed for climbing (harness, shoes, chalk, hardware, helmet?) • Inspect the climb/route map • Designate leader and belayer • Prepare rope • Determine to stick clip or spot first bolt • Close the system • Double-check • Communicate.

▼

On the climb: Manage hazards • Try hard • Fall? • Rest on the rope? • Employ sport climbing shenanigans? • Complete the climb? • Build an anchor? • Clean? • Lower? • Rappel?

At the belay: Select a device • Manage hazards • Manage the rope • Catch the leader? • Hold the leader while he/she rests? • Encourage • Pay attention • Help with shenanigans? • Lower?

▼

After the first lead: Pull the rope and leave/do not climb route again? • Pull the rope and lead (with or without quickdraws left in place)? • Toprope and lower? • Toprope and clean? w/ Lower? or Rappel??

Planning an Outing and Equipment

U nlike climbers who prepare for a toprope outing, sport climbers have different considerations
that should precede the actual outing. Their research
is slightly different because the thing they are preparing to do is different. Sport climbing is more difficult
to do in a large group setting because belayers and
leaders eventually pair off. Additionally, lead falls, by
their very nature, create hazards for passersby, proximal
climbing teams, and onlookers.

Sport climbers will need different equipment than
toproping teams because:

- Lead climbing will require the leader to connect
  the rope to protection components at increments
  throughout the climb.

- The leader will not require an extensive set of
  anchoring tools.

- The rope is asked to perform a more dynamic role
  in the climbing system.

- Belaying becomes a task that is much more
  difficult to master (requiring a more nuanced
  selection of tools).

Research

Guidebooks, online resources, and interpersonal
testimony are still a sport climber's main tools for

doing research on an area, a climb, or a community. Today, the care and thoroughness of guidebooks far exceeds the climate in which many of us learned to sport climb. However, guidebooks are as trapped in the unstated state of sport climbing as the climbing community itself, so readers of this text will need to learn to appreciate not only how a guidebook can be an enormous resource, but also how it can deceive as well as become dated. Similarly, online resources are often open sourced, and the ongoing commentary, photographs, and reporting allow a researcher to gain a more fluid consensus about the nature of a route. However, the general rabble surrounding a climb might not always reflect the reality, and online commentators are rarely as thorough or well informed as guidebook authors. Similarly, interpersonal testimony or beta can come in variable formats. A cowed climber will decry even the most reasonable leads, while his stalwart counterpart will boldly claim that a dangerous climb was not problem for her at all. Again, the real-time value of beta, even from a trustworthy source, is always tempered by the climber's unique perspective.

Guidebooks, online resources, and beta can also give a great history of the climb, including the date it was established, equipped, or first climbed. Many of the heartaches climbers experience relative to their reach should be anticipated with respect to this information. Tall first ascensionists make moves that seem reachy to everyone else, and shorter first ascensionists make moves that seem scrunched to everyone else. Additionally, the mythos or aura that surrounds a given climb is usually explicitly described in a guidebook, either through descriptions, star quality ratings, or photographs.

As a result of the sometimes conflicting, biased, or flexible nature of all the information that is available, a sport climbing researcher should learn to distinguish between objective data, subjective data, and consensus data when investigating a climb. Objective data is pure mathematical fact, indisputable and not open to interpretation. Subjective data is the opposite; it reflects the values, styles, strength/weaknesses, and aesthetics of the climber who provides the data. Consensus data is a slightly more reliable form of subjective data because so many people seem to agree with the subjective evaluation of a climb; it has the relative value of consensus. It is worth noting, however, that even a consensus of 5.14 climbers have a hard time evaluating the difficulty of a 5.8 climb for a 5.8 leader. Consensus data is still subjective in its own way.

Objective Data	Subjective Data	Consensus Data
• Route length	• Star rating	• Yosemite Decimal System (YDS)
• Number of bolts	• Reach dependence	• Protection quality/ rating
• Age/type of hardware	• Rock quality	
• Anchor type	• Endurance required	
• Aspect—sun/ weather exposure	• Scariness	
• Slope angle/ steepness	• Exposure	
• Rock type	• Experience quality—must be climbed!	
• Potential fall length	• Fall probability	

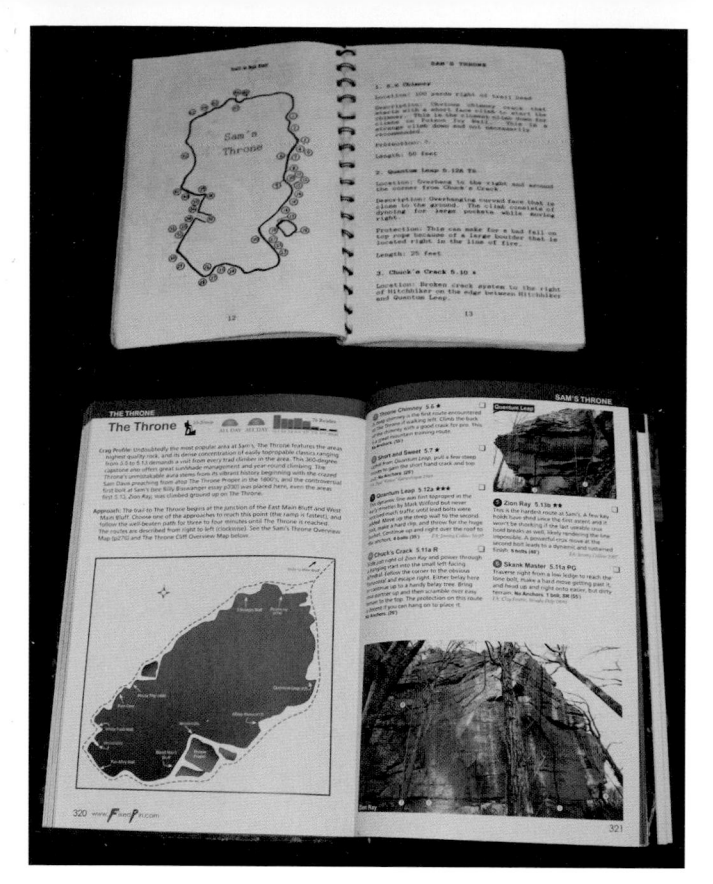

Over time, guidebooks have gotten more thorough and accurate, but they are not always a definitive resource. Sport climbers should combine guidebooks with other resources.

One of the most valuable calculations that most guidebooks allow the researcher to do is a quick bolt frequency calculation. The length of the climb divided by the number of bolts gives the researcher a crude calculation of the bolt frequency. For many climbers, this calculation alone disqualifies the climb as a sport climb.

Bolt Frequency Calculation

Guidebook states that Scimitar, 5.12a, Stone Mountain, North Carolina, has 9 bolts over 120 feet.

Length of Climb ÷ Number of Bolts = Bolt Frequency

120 feet ÷ 9 bolts = 13.3 feet/bolt

The lead climber had better be knowledgeable about and willing to experience 30-foot falls before attempting Scimitar. The bolt frequency suggests the potential for that kind of airtime, and it may be the fact that precludes the selection of the route in the first place.

Potential Fall Length versus Fall Probability

The cold and unavoidable calculus of potential fall length is often confused with the much squishier and unquantifiable notion of fall probability. With combined data, a sport climber should be able to make an informed choice in his/her research about the attractiveness of a given climb.

Potential fall length adds the greatest distance between two bolts on the route, doubles it, and adds rope elongation. Fall probability is less exact; it could depend entirely on the climber's fitness, ability to read a certain move at a certain time, and avoidance of fragile rock features, and on a host of unanticipated factors (wildlife, belayer interference, fatigue, weather, etc.). If most climbers tend to onsight the moves on a given section of a climb, it might be easy to ignore the potential fall length, but that doesn't dispute the cold, unequivocal consequence of the fall. Similarly, climbers who seek a climb that approaches the limits of what they can physically do, either because of endurance or free climbing difficulty, may be encouraged to take those falls when the potential fall lengths are minimal.

YDS

The Yosemite Decimal System is not objective data. One could easily argue that it was never designed to be. For a given climb, it represents the consensus understanding of the free climbing difficulties posed by the route. It is important to understand what is being aggregated when we refer to the consensus nature of a rating. The overall experience of a rock climb is being graded. That might mean that the nature of climbing from the bottom to the top has a cumulative difficulty. Or, it could easily mean that most of the climbing on a route is fairly negotiable, but short section(s) propose an aberrant problem that the climber must solve. As a result, enormously fit climbers tend to think endurance climbs are easy, while good boulderers are unimpressed with one-move wonders. Neither of them is right, and neither of them is wrong. However, their voices have to be averaged out with every other climber, and with every other predilection in movement, ability, and style. That is what consensus is supposed to mean.

Visual Mapping

Once all the information about a given climb has been gathered, it is wise to find a place, usually on the approach, where there is a vantage point over an entire rock climb. It is not uncommon to witness a sport

When visual mapping, be sure to

- Forecast the movement.

- Find all the bolts and the anchor. Is the type of anchor known?

- Get an idea about what holds will be used to clip the bolts.

- Find any undesirable hazards that the climb might pose.

- Release inherent hazards if *both* belaying *and* climbing are not set up and performed correctly. Falls double the distance from the last protection point are common and severe forces are generated.

climber "mapping" a climb from this vantage point. The aspiring leader has trained to see the cliff through the eyes of a lead climber and differentiate between sport climbs, trad climbs, and toprope-only climbs.

Leave No Trace

The Access Fund's Rock Project has done a superb job of educating American climbers about caring for the nation's crags in a conscientious and well-informed manner. Asking all climbers to make a pact to preserve the resource and our sense of community is something we shouldn't need to do, but as more and more climbers misbehave in the mountains, it's clear that each individual must make a commitment to care for the resource. Before a sport climbing outing, consider the main points of such a pact, ask the corresponding questions, and take appropriate action.

Pact	Research Question	Action
Respect other users.	Who are the other users?	If my activities are different from everyone else, I will integrate by . . .
Dispose of human waste properly.	Where am I going to pee and poop?	Bring disposal kits, find the communal pee spots, or climb near the toilets.
Park and camp in designated areas.	Where am I supposed to park at the cliff? Does the parking fill up?	Carpool and arrive early enough to get a spot. Have a plan B in case parking is full.
Stay on established trails.	Who maintains the trails? What do they look like?	Plan enough time to find the *established* trail.
Place gear and pads on durable surfaces.	What does the base of the climb look like?	Bring a bag that keeps all gear in a tidy pile.
Clean up chalk and tick marks.	Should I use chalk?	Bring a brush to clean excessive chalk.
Keep a low profile, minimizing group size and noise.	Should we split into small groups and reconvene later?	Figure out where to meet for lunch and/or where to meet afterward.
Pack out all trash, crash pads, and gear.	Where is the closest disposal site?	Bring trash bags and totes for litter.
Respect closures.	Is there a closure? Who owns the land?	Abide by closures and have a backup plan in case closure is unexpected.
Be an upstander, not a bystander.	What will I do if I see someone misbehaving? What will I do if I am accidentally misbehaving?	Rehearse being gentle and respectful while also being stern. Practice listening before speaking. Join the Access Fund, American Alpine Club, and/or local advocacy groups and coalitions.

Equipment

The equipment needed for a successful sport climbing outing can vary from one location to the next. The entire rack of sport climbing equipment, regardless of location, stems from an emphasis on leading more difficult routes. As a result, the team that has grown accustomed to packing for toproping outings will be able to leave some things at home, but they will probably need an entirely new set of tools for aspects of sport climbing that are dissimilar to toproping.

Rope. Sport climbing usually tests the limits of a climber's physical abilities, and shaving weight in every way possible is an attractive strategy. Plus, on average sport climbs tend to be steeper, so it becomes more common for rope to avoid rubbing against abrasive rock features entirely. The sport climbing leader, as a result, can logically experiment with ropes that might have a smaller diameter, less overall weight, and perhaps less durability than the ropes used in toproping. Today, single ropes designed for difficult sport climbing can be as thin as 8.8mm, and it is rare to find a proficient sport climbing team that favors anything thicker than 10mm. There are two predictable consequences to favoring a thinner rope: abrasive environments will quickly shred these thinner cords, and the rope elongation is usually greater. Sport climbers need to be aware of these factors when taking falls close to the ground or where there is ledge fall potential. That elongation can be more consequential, and the application of a thinner rope to abrasive terrain (lower angles, protrusions, or other interference) becomes unwise.

Similarly, rope length is a more deceptive criterion when sport climbing. When setting up a toprope, one usually discovers immediately that the rope is adequately long. But in sport climbing, a lack of research or foresight can result in a leader leading a climb with a rope that is too short. The discovery may not be made until the leader is several dozen feet above the ground, unable to lower the remaining distance. Many sport climbs soar through long sweeps of overhangs; some climbs are well over 100 feet. A prudent leader should know how long a climb is and how long the rope is before climbing, and it is best to know this information before arriving at the cliff that day. For sport climbing, the leader should pack a rope that is at least twice the length of the longest climb that day.

Quickdraws.

Since sport climbs are protected entirely by clipping the climbing rope to bolts, quickdraws are preferred. They are a necessity, and a sport climber will need to appreciate the varieties of carabiners available, the lengths available, and how many to bring along.

To lead a climb, the leader will need enough quickdraws to clip every bolt and perhaps the anchor bolts as well. So, it is important to know how many bolts are on the longest climb one intends to do on a given day. Additionally,

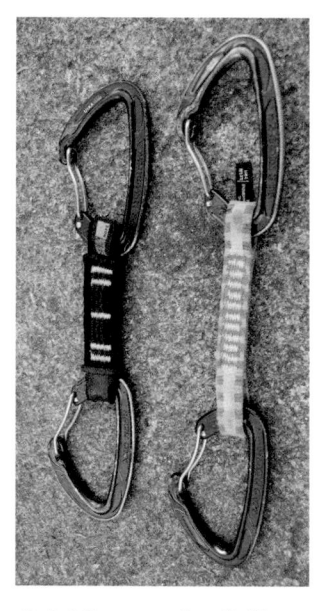

Quickdraws: nylon (left) and UHMWP (right). Note the size and material differences as well as the direction and orientation of the carabiners.

because quickdraws are usually positioned on the harness alternately on the right and left sides, it is conceivable that a lead climber may find him/herself in a position where clips from the right side predominate. As a result, having a few extra quickdraws on each side prepares a leader to deal with whatever spread of clips he/she actually encounters when first attempting to lead a climb. If a climb has ten bolts, for example, and the leader carries fourteen quickdraws split between the right and left sides of the harness, seven out of ten clips could conveniently be positioned on one side or the other. Believe it or not, there are climbs that happen this way, and having those extra quickdraws on one side may make the difference between an onsight and a whipper.

Carabiners.

Using a pair of non-locking carabiners and a sling to connect/attach a bolt to a climbing rope is an ancient practice in lead climbing. Early sport climbing followed this practice or attached the rope to a bolt with carabiner(s) solely. In sport climbing, however, this connection

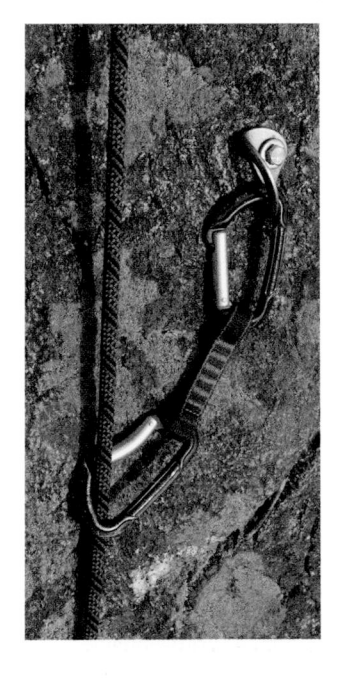

Carabiner gate styles on a quickdraw: straight gate connects to bolt, bent gate is for the rope and easier clipping.

became both ubiquitous and frequent, so manufacturers began producing preassembled pairs of carabiners with shorter and often more rigid, easier to clip textiles in a myriad of colors, shapes, sizes, materials, carabiner combinations, and intended uses.

Historically, a sling could be used to combine any pair of carabiners into a runner, and therefore selecting and combining those two runner carabiners was a decision left to the leader. But since manufacturers now preassemble quickdraws, those choices are less available. Most of the time, however, a preassembled quickdraw combines two carabiners that are ideally suited for clipping the bolt on one side and the rope on the other.

Quickdraw textile. The textile between two carabiners for most quickdraws is approximately 12cm, but longer runners may be up to 17cm. It is rare to find preassembled quickdraws in lengths that exceed 17cm. The materials used to construct the runners are more widely variable, but the two main categories are nylon and an ultra-high-molecular-weight polyethylene (UHMWP) like Spectra or Dyneema. *Climbing: Gym to Rock* covers these in more detail. As always, know your materials and use them per the manufacturers' specifications.

Belay device. When packing a belay device, there are two options, and in almost every circumstance it is advisable to bring both. An ABD (Assisted Braking Device) is a great selection when the leader falls repeatedly, when working a climb, or when rockfall could incapacitate the belayer. But, alone, an ABD is not always the best tool for cleaning an anchor and descending via rappel. Even though this cleaning sequence should be rare, it does occur, and an MBD (Manual Braking Device) will be needed. However, if minimizing the overall pack size and equipment available is an absolute

Textile/Soft Good Attachments

The following definitions can add some clarity to understanding soft goods (aka textiles) used as attachments.

- **Quickdraw:** A rigid or semirigid textile with two carabiners, one on each end. One of these carabiners is typically held in place tightly to facilitate clipping.

- **Runner:** A sling with two carabiners, one on each end. The sling used to make a runner is usually shortened (aka extendable runner or alpine quickdraw). When done properly, you can unclip any two strands (keep one in the carabiner!) to extend back to full length.

- **Sling:** A sewn or tied loop of a flat textile (nylon or UHMWP [*ultra high molecular weight polyethylene*]). Shoulder (standard) length and double length are common.

Be conscious of sewn joints (bar tacks) and knotted joints in these attachments. Ideally they are kept off of components and carabiners and are not in any new knots that may be created. Also beware of quickdraw accessories (usually some sort of rubber) that help stabilize the clipping carabiner. These have been misused with tragic results. Ensure that carabiners are properly through the quickdraw's soft good material, not just the rubber stabilizer.

Belay devices. Clockwise from top: ABD, Pinch, and MBD

priority for the climbing team, to ease a long hike or strenuous approach, for example, there are hybrid devices that can split the difference between an MBD and an ABD. Extra-grabbing Pinch devices, like the Mega Jul, CT Alpine Up, or the Mammut Alpine Smart, can give a smooth rope feed, a reliable grab for working a route, and a margin of error if the belayer is compromised.

Harness. Sport climbing made a noticeable impact on harness manufacture and design. Today, it is not uncommon for many climbers to have more than one harness, and their sport climbing harness is usually selected for some specific criteria. First, a sport climbing harness needs only enough gear loops to carry quickdraws, and perhaps a few small items needed for cleaning. So, it is conceivable that the harness will have only two gear loops (although most have four). How you carry is also a factor. When climbing at the peak of one's ability, it might be smart to have as light a harness as possible. Selecting a lightweight model, with fewer gear loops, therefore might be advisable. Of course, the harness might also hold a climber through multiple lead

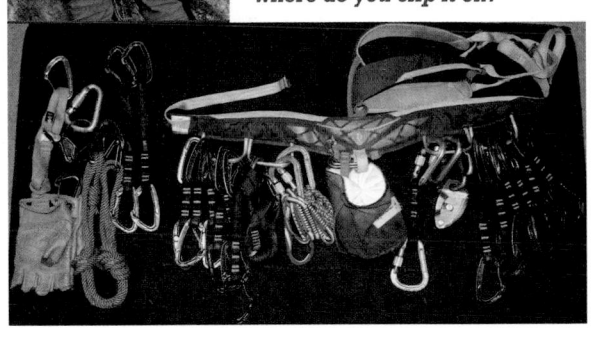

A harness at a personal baseline—tailored and "standardized" to the individual's needs/style and the route. The climber is prepared, organized, and ready to go sport climbing, having asked these questions: How do you clip it on, what do you clip it on, and where do you clip it on?

falls, both climbing and belaying. So, a balance between comfort and lightweight designs should be struck.

Shoes. Toproping is usually an introduction to climbing as well as climbing movement, so an introductory pair of climbing shoes is usually the way to go (a comfortable all-arounder with a flat last). In sport climbing, however, a more aggressive shoe with a more aggressive fit can have measureable advantages in performance. For overhanging climbs, a tight downturned shoe allows the climber to pull in with the toes, lock in the heel, and take weight off of the arms. On a difficult face climb, small edges can be asked to hold the climber's entire body weight. The specialization of the movement required to sport climb at a high level usually requires specialized footwear, too, so pack shoes that do the job(s).

Rockfall Likelihood Questionnaire

- Is there evidence of rockfall at the base of the cliff?

- Does the rock look crumbly and fragile in places that I can see?

- Is there more cliff above the anchors?

- Is everyone else wearing a helmet?

- Is the cliff new, or have people been sport climbing here for more than ten years?

- Are there people on top of the cliff that might dislodge rocks and debris?

- Are there climbers or challenges present that increase the likelihood of equipment dropping?

If the answer to any of these questions is yes, helmet use is advisable.

Helmet. In sport climbing, helmet use is not as common as it is in other disciplines of climbing, and the climber must make a very careful choice. Clipping bolts and wearing a helmet—not mutually exclusive!

If one chooses not to wear a helmet, hopefully there are some qualifying criteria in place. Is there a proven unlikelihood of rockfall events? Not many cliffs in the United States meet that criterion.

It might also be valuable to consider a professional instructor's perspective on helmet use. Perhaps the best question sport climbers should ask themselves is: If this is a risk professional instructors, with years of insight and experience, cannot even afford to calculate, am I willing to make a different decision?

Sport Climbing Specific

Gloves. Many sport climbers like to belay with gloves and have their belayer use gloves. Gloves enhance a belayer's grip and add security to the brake position during a lead fall. They also save the skin and hands for climbing.

Belay glasses. Another sign of sport climbing's evolution is belay glasses. These are becoming more and more common at the cliff. Users swear they increase ergonomics, again saving the body for climbing, and provide better views of the leader.

Knee/thigh pads. These specialized sticky, rubber-coated sleeves are common at areas where knee bars, knee scums, and other leg jamming or smearing is inherent in the style of climbing. A "trick to stick" on the climb.

Fancy quickdraws. These specialized quickdraws are designed to ease clipping. One such design holds the gate open, so the rope can be dropped in. Once this occurs the gate closes.

An array of specialized equipment for sport climbing.

Stick clipping is a part of sport climbing and a great risk-management tool. Some routes are equipped with a high first bolt with this practice in mind.

Stick clip. Using a stick clip to connect a quick-draw and rope to the first bolt is becoming the most common practice in sport climbing. If it were a universal practice, climbers would enjoy greater protection from groundfall, the first bolts of sport climbs could be higher (resulting in fewer bolts overall), and every climbing team could avoid having to fashion a stick clip from limbs and branches.

Sport Climbing Kit List

Standard sport rack and more for a day of sport climbing.

- Quickdraws
- Stick clip
- Locking carabiners
- Belay device(s)
- Climbing shoes
- Anchor-building materials
- First aid kit
- Phone
- Extra clothing
- Food/water
- Belay gloves
- Guidebook
- Specialized equipment: kneepads, belay glasses, fancy quickdraws

Guiding Principles of Equipment Use

- Take care of it: Store wisely and inspect.
- Heed the lifespan based on the manufacturer's recommendation or failed inspection.
- Know the materials: What is your equipment made of?
- What are their preferred applications?
- Use per the manufacturer's specifications!

CHAPTER 3

The Sport Climb: Base, Protection, and Anchor

I n this chapter we will further explore the features and the hardware that distinguish a sport climb from any other lead climb. We will focus on the overall setting and base of the climb at first, but then we will look at the hardware and protection points that secure a lead climber. Lastly, we'll look at the anchor bolts. Taken together, these parts constitute a sport climb, and a conversation about how to climb these climbs won't be productive if we don't know what exactly we are talking about.

The Base

While we tend to think of climbing, clipping the bolts, and setting the anchor as the base of the climb is at least as important as those more obvious features. Aside from all the concerns the climbing team might have for managing their belongings or addressing LNT principles, the base of the climb is where the belayer will be. What's more, if there is a catastrophic failure of the protection system, the base is where the leader is likely to end up. So, it is very much a part of the climb. In preparation for any climb, the climber and the belayer must establish a locker room for their belongings, a belay position, and a landing zone(s) for the lowering leader or tumbling rope.

A locker room is a place where backpacks and belongings can be discretely sorted and stowed while the climbing team racks up, changes apparel and

This belayer has positioned the rope on her brake hand side and tried to find a spot where the leader will not fall directly on her head.

footwear, and eats and drinks. Organize your gear and keep it out of everyone's way!

Once equipment and backpacks are stowed, the positions of the rope and the belay team are important. The belay must find a place to stack the rope, so that it feeds directly to his/her brake hand position without getting entangled in vegetation or equipment. We will discuss the position of the belay at length in chapter 4, but for now we will say that it is a greater priority than the position of the locker room. We might find any number of places to put our stuff, but there are usually only one or two good places to belay a leader.

Landing Zones

Many climbers forget, until the last minute, that the fall line of an anchor (the fall line for lowering from the top) and the fall line of every bolt along the way are not always the same. Climbers can be lowered into treetops or poison ivy thickets, and falling ropes can ensnare branches and/or fall into streambeds.

Fixed Protection: The Bolts

The term *fixed* relates to the permanent nature of these protection components. Once placed, they remain fixed in place. When sport climbing, the climber expects to utilize a plethora of modern bolts in a variety of designs, shapes, and sizes. Pitons, while a type of fixed protection one should be aware of, are not part of sport climbing and will not be discussed in detail. The sport climber should not expect to interact with anything other than modern bolts.

There are likely land management rules and regulations as well as responsible usage ethics to govern the use of fixed protection at a climbing area. Fixed protection is not allowed in some areas; in other areas a particular process must be followed (permit, application, etc.) or particular methods may be required for installing fixed protection (e.g., hand drilling). For the purposes of this text, we will resist the temptation to delve into establishing sport climbs, or how to join efforts to maintain and replace fixed protection. As previously stated, those efforts are best rejoined with communal expertise, permission, and consensus. We will focus this chapter on using and evaluating the bolts, not necessarily establishing or maintaining them. You should learn more about a climbing area in advance, including how bolts are established and maintained; check with the land managers, local climbing groups, and the Access Fund for guidance and answers to questions on fixed protection (and a host of other topics).

If a sport climber is well informed and has done good research prior to a climb, there should be a clear expectation of how many bolts he/she will see on a given lead. The only remaining question becomes assessing bolts as protection components during a lead climb or when building an anchor. Since the origins and history of a bolt are not always obvious to the naked eye, a leader should be able to quickly assess the value of a bolt. Remember, using bolts at a sport climbing area should be a risk management tool that deemphasizes physical risk and complex technical risk. A sport climbing outing should focus on movement and athleticism; utilizing protection should not be a big leap of faith. But before a leader can evaluate a bolt, it's important to understand what he/she is looking at. This process starts with an understanding of

An array of bolts. At the center is a modern stainless steel expansion bolt with a stainless steel hanger. Some are painted to blend in with the rock, a low-impact practice.

the fixed bolt options you may find at a cliff and what makes these options viable for managing risk.

There are two main types of modern bolts: mechanical bolts and glue-ins. Mechanical bolts expand in some mechanical fashion when a metal hanger is tightened into place. Their holding power is derived from the mechanical expansion of a sleeve as the bolt is tightened. Glue-ins are exactly what one would expect: round stocked bolts and cylindrical shafts that are covered in glue and inserted into a drilled hole; the glue chemically bonds to the rock and the bolt as it dries, hardens, and slightly expands.

A mechanical bolt typically consists of two parts: a hanger resting on the surface of the rock with a perpendicular opening that facilitates attachments via carabiners, and some sort of metal bolt inserted into a drilled hole in the rock. There are exceptions to this description, the most common of which is a glue-in bolt.

Being able to recognize modern bolts and hangers is an important skill, but it can be difficult at first. Luckily, there are not that many kinds common to

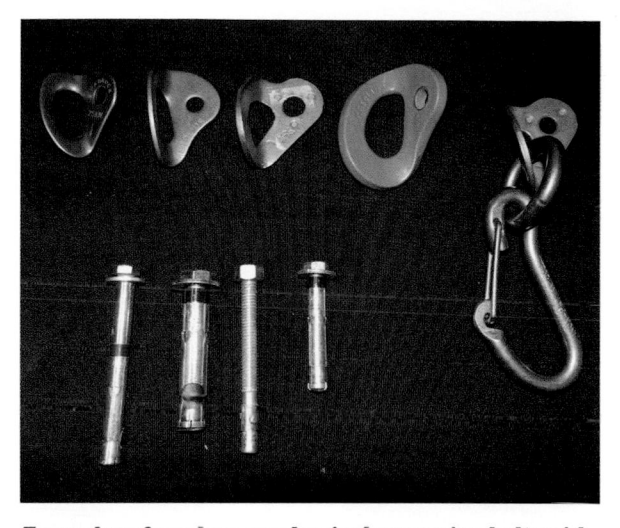

Examples of modern mechanical expansion bolts with modern hangers.

"I had become convinced of the superiority of glue-in bolts, but when bolting steep routes at the Red, I realized how difficult they were to use in overhanging rock. I used all the available glue-in designs and tricks to keep them in the rock while the glue set, but when one fell out above me and hit me in the head, I realized there had to be a better design. I was inspired by how pitons work, and also wanted to combine some open space in the shaft of the bolt so that the glue could encase the bolt instead of just harden around its exterior. My solution was the tapered wave design, which produces resistance to pull-out before the glue sets as well as tremendous strength with fully cured glue."

—Isaac Heacock, inventor of the Wave Bolt

modern sport climbing anymore. Bolt replacement initiatives and first ascensionists alike tend to gravitate toward a few different proven varieties, and they are easy to recognize.

Modern Glue-in Bolts

The Wave Bolt, produced by ClimbTech, is a one-piece bolt that is a glue-in but also has expansion/ wedging action. The Twisted Leg Bolt, produced by Bolt Products, is also popular on many cliffs and crags. Petzl glue-ins are tried-and-true standards in much of Europe, and they were some of the first glue-in bolts in the United States.

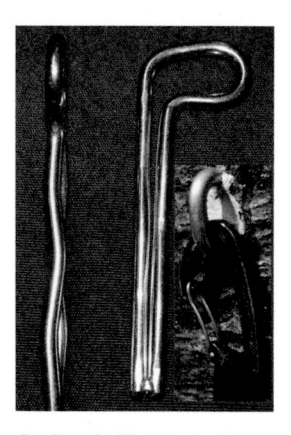

A glue-in Wave Bolt in profile and in action.

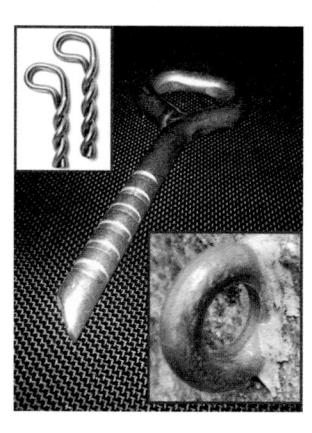

Other modern glue-in bolts, including a Twisted Leg, in the rock and out.

Random "Bolts"

There are other fixed protection types similar to bolts described here that you may encounter. Like the modern and common bolts, they are hammered, glued, and/or somehow expand in the rock. The assessment tools outlined here can help you judge their viability.

Properly installed modern bolts and hangers are at the core of sport climbing. However, even modern equipment is subject to age degradation and environmental stresses (freeze, thaw, moisture, salt air, rock type, etc.).

So, what does a savvy sport climber look for?

- Modern bolt type, not too old, that is properly tightened/glued

- Acceptable type, diameter, and length for rock type/hardness

- Bolt placed into quality rock, perpendicular to the plane of rock

- Modern hangers made by a known manufacturer with an imprinted strength rating. They do not spin, do make full contact with the rock below, and are oriented in the appropriate direction of pull.

- Hangers and bolts that are designed by the manufacturer for rock climbing—not hardware store or industrial types!

- Stainless steel construction (titanium in marine environments)

- No cracks, rust, pitting/corrosion, damage, etc.

Dubious Bolts

Bolting is not simple or easy; it is a lot of hard work that requires planning and precision. In addition to the time, effort, and skill required, there is an expense.

Bolting Errors

- Drilled hole is an incorrect depth.

- Drilled hole is an incorrect diameter.

- Drilled hole is dirty.

- Rock quality is poor.

- Expansion mechanism is over- or undertightened.

- Mixed metal utilized between bolt and hanger—this leads to more rapid galvanic corrosion.

- Glue volume or composition is incorrect.

- Glue does not adhere properly.

The hardware and equipment needed to place a modern bolt are not cheap! The savvy sport climber will treat all bolts with care and appreciate the efforts of the installer and support these efforts when possible. The climber also should be aware of the pitfalls and potential errors inherent in the installation process. This helps with onsite assessment by a climber. Excessive wear, spinning hangers, and loose bolts should be immediately concerning.

The following list provides some, but not all, examples of antiquated bolts and hangers. Investigate any suspect/unknown bolts and hangers further.

Low-strength antiquated bolts

¼-inch-diameter compression buttonhead

¼-inch-diameter compression with nut

Self-drilling expansion

Buttonhead nail-in

Taper-style nail-in or screw-in

Nail Star Drive—Star Dryvins

Torqueing-style bolts

Drop-in

Stud

Bad hangers

Modified Lost Arrow piton

Old Thin SMC (there are newer ones that meet modern standards)

Pull-tab style

Homemade angle iron/aluminum

Old Leeper hanger

Examples of vintage bolts and hangers, low in protection value/security.

Examples of some questionable modern bolts found on popular sport climbs, including a loose nut/hanger and a rusted nut/bolt (which should be evaluated for further galvanic corrosion).

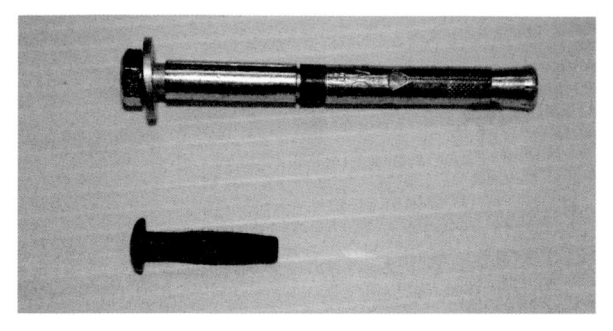

Which one would you rather clip? Learn to identify bolts!

Fixed Draws

A final attachment consideration that you will likely come across when sport climbing is a fixed draw. These are quickdraws that are in place when you arrive at the crag. They are already attached to the bolts and awaiting your climb; you will only need to clip the rope into them. There are a variety of reasons they would be present (steep climb, project in progress, etc.), though experienced climbers debate the practice all the time. It is important to understand some of the risks associated with using them. First, you likely will not know who left them there and how long they have been in place. Depending on the sport climbing venue, there may be dedicated locals who "manage" this equipment or there may not be. Second, the parts may not be in prime condition. The two things, in addition to the fixed protection, to carefully evaluate are the textile and carabiners. Ultraviolet light can degrade textiles quickly. Textiles left outside can lose their strength quickly. Carabiners on fixed draws can experience lots of wear if there are repeated lowers off of them. This is common at the crux bolt. Rope

Fixed draws on sport climbs. On the right are permadraws, perhaps the longest-lasting fixed draws! Despite the name, they, like all fixed draws, should be assessed at each use.

grooves can happen surprisingly quickly in environments with sand or coarse soils. Inspect fixed draws. To counter some of these hazards, fixed draws made without textiles and with harder metals (steel) less prone to wear are being utilized in some places. Regardless of their construction, be sure to inspect fixed draws carefully.

The Anchors

The final portion of a sport climb is the anchor. Its components are the same protection bolts we have discussed up to this point, but there are at least two of them. Most noticeably, anchor bolts will have different kinds of hangers, an array of chain or quick (rapid) links, or round rappel rings to facilitate the utilization of the anchor. A smooth focal/master point(s), of some form or another, differentiates anchor bolts from protection bolts. The components should each be evaluated as described above. Anchors with multiple parts can further complicate this evaluation process (and be of mixed metal types—beware!). Evaluate carefully!

The focal/master point(s) can be found in three main categories:

1. Small opening (fits single-strand rope end only)

Small-opening fixed anchors.

2. Large opening (fits bight of rope)—double or single ring (if single, usually 50kN master point)

3. Quick/direct (rope can be clipped)

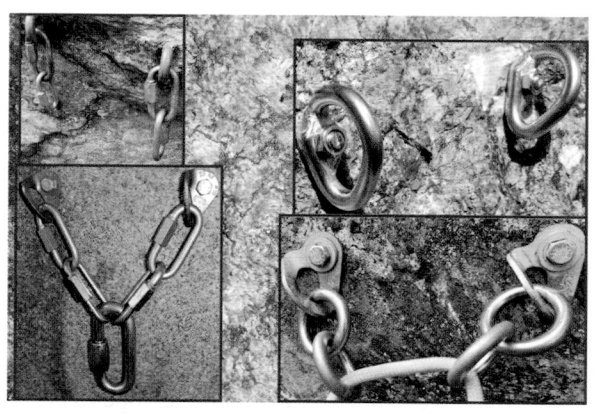

Large-opening fixed anchors.

Quick/direct fixed anchors.

Because there are different kinds of anchor configurations, it may be baffling for sport climbers to decide how to anchor at the top of the cliff. There are a few common strategies, and they range from simple to complex (see chapter 7).

Anchor bolts, all their parts, and their smooth focal point(s) are all points of inspection and potential failure. When in doubt about these extra pieces, rig your own anchor directly to the bolts and the rope, even if you need to leave it. You are well worth the few dollars to replace some slings and carabiners.

It is helpful to sort fixed anchors into the three aforementioned categories. These categories/styles are based on the size/nature of the opening that the rope can be attached to/passed through. A small-opening fixed anchor allows only a single-strand rope end to be passed through it. A large-opening fixed anchor allows a bight of rope to be passed through it. A quick/direct fixed anchor allows the rope to be clipped into it directly.

A common type of quick/direct anchor, the cold shut, was very common in the earlier days of sport climbing. Essentially the rope was just dropped into two of these for anchoring. Sometimes they were homemade or hardware store versions. Cold shuts were lower security and always seemed worn. Be aware of and closely evaluate cold shuts; they push the definition of *modern*. Using them for lowering did not require any technical procedures, and they were one piece and contained no moving parts. The latter characteristics were great, and this type of

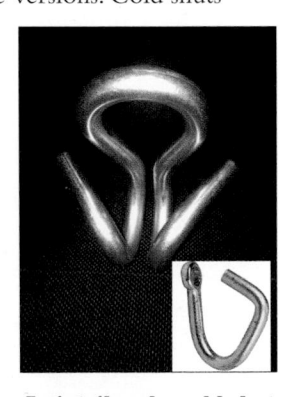

A pigtail and a cold shut.

quick/direct fixed anchor may be seeing a resurgence with the "pigtail." Common in Europe, this anchor requires the rope to be deliberately circled through to its resting point. Thus additional security is not sacrificed for simplicity as with the cold shut.

Toproping and Fixed Anchors

Do not toprope through fixed anchors. The rope rubbing under tension from lowers and falls can rapidly wear out the fixed anchor. If protracted toprope sessions are the objective, set up one of the appropriate anchors mentioned in chapter 7 and clean them as outlined in chapter 8 when the toproping is complete. Using fixed anchors in this low impact, LNT manner is sound practice to increase the lifespan of fixed protection that sport climbers rely on.

PLEASE
do not top rope
through the fixed
gear

Use your own gear for top ropes, then have the last climber lower or rappel.

The fixed anchors are expensive and wear out quickly. If you see questionable hardware, leave gear and a note as necessary. Once notified, individuals will take action.
Thanks.

Notice the wear! A sign encourages topropers to use their own equipment.

Belaying

As revolutionary as it was, sport climbing did not amend the fundamental principles of belaying. Those principles carried into sport climbing, and they proved themselves consistently in yet another context. To review, belaying, in all contexts, is fundamentally sound if

- The rope is always firmly gripped by at least one brake hand.

- Anytime the brake hand is sliding on the rope, or making a transition, the rope is in the position of maximum friction, also known as the braking plane.

- The limbs and extremities are positioned naturally, according to the body's natural strength.

There are some additional considerations when belaying for a leader on a sport climb. The lead climber on a sport climb will predictably create two circumstances that demand a vastly different skill set from the belayer. If the leader really is pushing his/her physical abilities, he/she is likely to fall frequently. Second, the nature of the lead fall creates substantially greater forces than a toprope. As a corollary to these two realities, lead belayers become more interactive than a toprope belayer. Toprope belayers mindlessly reel in slack and then eventually lower. Meanwhile, lead belayers give slack, compensate for excess slack, and assert an aggressive counterweight so the leader can rest, and they must rapidly pay out and take in slack at varying rates to mitigate fall consequences. It can be exhausting.

In this chapter we will discuss the five critical considerations in lead belaying:

1. Setup and positioning
2. Communication
3. Giving slack
4. Compensating
5. Catching falls

Setup and Positioning

The bottom of a climb, where the belayer stands, is an intrinsic part of a sport climb. The position of the rope stack should allow the belayer to easily access the entire length of rope on his/her brake hand side.

If the tail of the rope is not being used by the belayer, a knot should visibly close the system for

A savvy setup for sport climbing.

all viewers. A rope mat, bag, or bucket can be handy tools to keep the rope out of dirt or mud. Then, the belayer must find a position relative to the rope stack that allows the belayer to spot the leader until the first bolt is clipped, keep the standing end of the rope from tripping the leader, and avoid a collision with the falling leader. For many belayers, all those criteria cannot be met if a ground anchor is used. For others, effective counterweight and a stable secure belay to catch falls is not even possible without a ground anchor. So, there are variables that any belayer must account for when designating the position of the belay.

When should I use a ground/bottom anchor? When a climber and belayer have a weight discrepancy that is greater than 40 percent, the use of a ground anchor is advisable. In other words, if a lead climber weighs 100 pounds, the belayer should weigh at least 60 pounds. Those two climbers have a 40 percent weight discrepancy.

Where should I ground anchor? Belayers should strive to ground anchor at a point that is 10 to 20 degrees back out of line with the fall line of the first bolt. Or, somewhere between the fall line of the first bolt and the base of the cliff.

When a ground anchor is used, the location should position the belayer such that the falling leader doesn't land directly on the belayer's head, but also in a position where falls later on during the lead do not result in a dramatic outward pull on the first bolt or the quickdraw. The deep grooves that many fixed carabiners on the first bolts of sport climbs exhibit is partially due to the position of the belay team.

On a vertical or low-angled sport climb, there is no distance between the fall line of the bolt and the

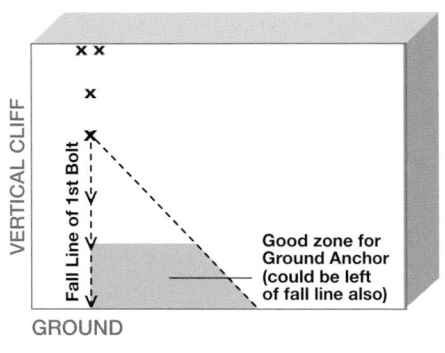

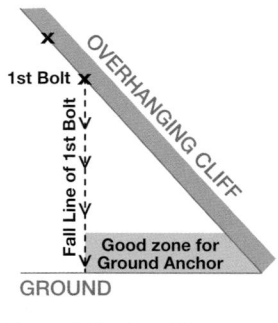

Ground Anchor Diagram

base of the cliff. As a result, the belay should ground anchor 10 to 20 degrees right or left of that fall line.

How should I ground/bottom anchor?

Remember that a ground anchor serves as ballast to a belayer's body weight. So, the criteria that toproping teams prioritize when building anchors (to utilize for climbing) at the top of the cliff are less vital. There are numerous ways to anchor a belayer. The belay team will need to find something that can hold some force, a protection component. Then, the team will need some material to attach to the component, an attachment tool. Trees (even smaller ones), rocks and boulders, other climbers, even a group of backpacks can all serve as valuable protection components for a sport climbing bottom anchor. The climbing rope, slings, or cordellette are common attachment tools. Use the component and the attachment tool to create a bottom anchor with a master point. The belayer should connect this master point to the belay loop with a locking carabiner. This should be connected in such a way that it is below the belay device and on the brake hand side. The anchor,

The yellow line represents the ABC line (or anchor–belayer–climber). The climber's force on the belayer is directed through the first bolt.

A sport climber's belayer anchored with a doubled-up cordellette around a rock component. He is attached to this anchor with his climbing rope tie in, cloved hitched to it via a locking carabiner.

the belayer, and the first bolt (ABC line) should be positioned in a straight line, such that the falling climber's weight (force transmitted through the first bolt) loads the belayer and the ground anchor simultaneously. The ultimate goal is to ensure a belay is sound, stable, and secure. There should be no dramatic lifting or compromising of the belay.

Communication

The belay commands familiar to any toproping party will also suffice in sport climbing. Communication allows for the unambiguous confirmation that the belayer is belaying, the climber is climbing, and the system has been secured and double-checked. Sport climbing tends to open up new circumstances and it therefore requires an emphasis on precise and unambiguous communication. For example, when the toprope climber calls "Take" or "Tension," a belayer may assert an aggressive counterweight and pull all the latent elasticity (stretch) out of the toprope system. In sport climbing, if the belayer does not aggressively pull the latent elasticity out of the system, the leader will slide down away from the quickdraw, which at that point indicates a high point. In toproping, when a climber indicates "Falling," there is little for the belayer to do but maintain the brake and become a counterweight. But in sport climbing, announcing a fall communicates that a belayer is about to experience a large dynamic force. Lastly, the communication at the anchor is supremely important, and many unfortunate accidents have occurred because of miscommunications during anchoring or cleaning. Suffice it to say, before a leader leads, there should be a clear plan of action for what will happen at the belay. Most of the time the leader will anchor and then be lowered, so there is no need for extraneous (and confusing) communication.

Giving Slack

Paying out an adequate amount of slack is a delicate estimation. Experience as a lead climber usually forges a better belayer, because the belayer has a stronger experiential instinct for what enables the lead, what encourages the leader, and the things that completely disable, encumber, and jeopardize a successful lead. The right amount of slack is just right; it is neither too tight nor too loose. One of the best ways to learn is to solicit running feedback from an experienced belayer, while lead belaying. It might be advisable to put the leader on a warmup climb or one well within his/her abilities first. It should be practiced, for each belay device you plan to use, in advance and in no-consequence settings.

With different devices, giving slack is slightly different.

With a Manual Braking Device (MBD), aka tuber/plate/aperture. Slide non-brake hand toward device, brake hand away. Move both hands up/forward to get rope through the device and to the climber. Be ready to repeat or to PBUS back in the excess slack. This is constant as the climber advances upward. When a leader is clipping, you may have to repeat giving slack quickly in large armloads two to three times, perhaps take a step forward, and then immediately remove excess slack via PBUS after the clip.

Giving slack with an MBD. Just one of the armloads of slack required during a sport climb.

Common MBD Belaying Errors

- Losing control of brake on slack feeding
- Shorting the leader during a clip/pulling the leader
- Pinching hand in device when braking

With an ABD. Use the manufacturer's method for maintaining brake and giving slack. This varies from

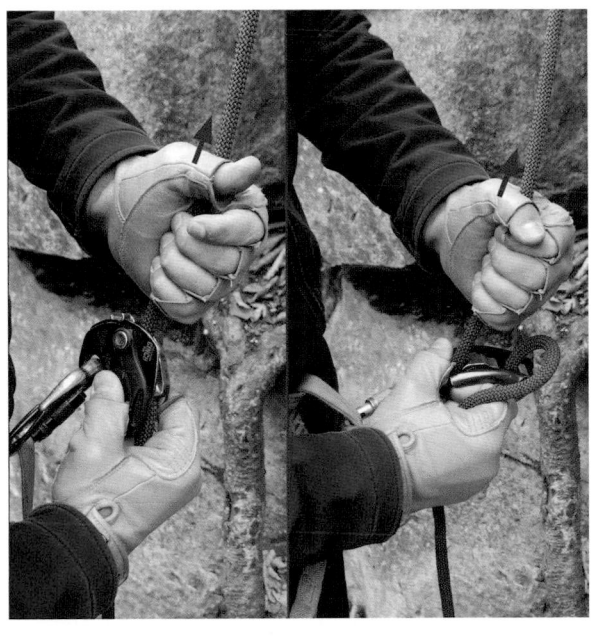

Giving slack to a sport climb leader with two different ABDs. Know the correct method and never let go of the brake strand of the rope!

device to device, but usually involves a procedure that defeats the camming mechanism while maintaining control of the brake.

Common ABD Belaying Errors

- Losing control of brake on slack feeding

- Assuming assisted braking is foolproof and hands-free

    - Rope has to be correctly inserted and be of the right diameter range. Even when within the manufacturer's usable range, skinny ropes perform differently.

    - Light climbers can affect the assisted function.

    - Rope drag and rope friction routes can affect the assisted function.

    - Light hangs (not falls) may not engage cam.

- Shorting the leader during a clip/pulling the leader

- Lowering too fast/losing control

- Not using PBUS brake position to help engage assisted function

- Removing brake hand without a catastrophe knot/system close

With a pinch device. Use the manufacturer's method for maintaining brake and giving slack. This varies from device to device, but usually involves a procedure that reverses/releases the pinch while maintaining control of the brake.

Giving slack to a sport climb leader with a Pinch device.

Common Pinch Device Belaying Errors

- Losing control on slack feeding

- Shorting the leader during a clip/pulling the leader

- Lowering too fast/losing control

- Removing brake hand without a catastrophe knot/system close

- Incorrectly inserting rope

- Lowering climber too fast/losing control

- Using rope of inappropriate diameter for device

Rappelling *may or may not* need a backup depending on model and manufacturer.

Compensating

Many experienced belayers forget to articulate, when they teach others, that compensating is a huge part of lead belaying. Lead belayers must learn to instantly and instinctively transition between giving and taking slack. When a leader is struggling to clip a rope, slack is pulled into the system; the slack is sometimes dropped before a successful clip, and the leader desperately pulls the slack up again. At any time the leader could fall. So, the hyper-reactive belayer should give slack, then quickly take slack, then quickly give slack, and perhaps be ready to take in some slack while the leader is falling.

Similarly, when leaders pull long arm lengths of slack into the belay system and clip far above their heads, there is a moment when they enjoy a 2- to 4-foot toprope. The belayer, as a result, must give slack, take in a little slack, and then seamlessly transition to giving again as the leader passes the quickdraw. Then, there is the event wherein the leader clips, then downclimbs some distance to recoup a good rest. The belayer must pay out slack for the clip, continue to pay out slack for the downclimb, then take in slack when the leader reascends to the high point, and seamlessly transition to giving slack again once the leader passes the quickdraw. Lastly, after a lead fall, a leader often wants to use the rope (via batmanning or boinking, see Chapter 9) to climb back up to the high point, so the lead belayer has to take in slack in fitful body-weighted increments while the leader climbs back up to his/her high point.

Point is, lead belaying is not just giving slack and catching falls. It is interactive, and it requires insight into the experience of leading as well as the utmost vigilance, preparedness, and attentiveness.

Catching Falls

There is a surprising amount of rhetoric surrounding the notion of a "soft catch," and it is unnerving to observe that this notion is emphasized before the plain skill of catch. Many well-intentioned novice lead belayers have allowed leaders to hit the ground or a ledge, as they attempt to soften a catch. Unless belayers are unnecessarily ground anchored, most lead falls are soft, because the force generated by the leader's falling bodyweight tends to dislodge the belayer no matter what he/she does.

So, a better tactic for novice lead belayers is to learn to become what they will most likely be, no matter what: a dynamic counterweight. When a leader falls, the force on the belayer is startling and abrupt, and it can be scary until it is familiar. Belayers must accept that no force or action can restrain them when the leader falls, nor would they want it to. Instead, they must accept the inevitability of the small ride they are about to take, and just ride it until it stops. While they are riding, belayers can use their legs and their feet to push off the wall, to avoid abrasions and impacts, all the while maintaining the brake position and the catch. As the leader decelerates, the belayer will eventually halt as well, and he/she must lower his/her now-suspended counterweight back to the ground to begin the process anew.

Once belayers are familiarized and competent with this reality, the "catching a fall" reality, it might be time to experiment with the nuanced and advanced skill of incrementally and intentionally increasing the length of a lead fall so that the lead climber can drop harmlessly into space, clear a roof, or avoid incidental impact from a ledge or protrusion. But it would be foolish to practice these skills until the more basic competence (catching a fall consistently) is achieved.

A Good Sport Climbing Belayer:

- Gives the climber constant and complete focus during all four phases of a lead climb: prelead, lead, anchor, postlead (lower, second, etc.)

- Ensures that preclimb checks (personal, partner, and system) are thoroughly performed

- Assesses if a backup belayer or bottom anchor is needed

- Spots a climber prior to the first clip when necessary

- Is always aware of the fall path of the climber

- Moves the rope out of the climber's way during the spotting phase or initial part of the climb

- Never lets go of the brake strand of the rope

- Can constantly manage the rope: without pulling the climber, can feed out slack, take up slack, feed out large amounts of slack at clips, and then take it in rapidly, keeping slack to a minimum

  - Is smooth, efficient, and effective, offering just the right amount of slack

  - Understands how moving away lessens slack and moving closer increases slack during a climb

- Can brake and hold a lead fall at all times

  - Is prepared with a stance and location to do so—position of function

  - Realizes comfort and location are secondary to the necessity of maintaining a good belay for the leader

- Lowers a climber at a reasonable speed in a safe manner

- Helps the lead climber in risk management: Does the climber have what he/she needs? Are clips good? Is the rope running in a dangerous manner (e.g., behind a leg)? Is protection adequate? etc.

CHAPTER 5

Clipping

Clipping is one of the nonnegotiable chores on a sport climb. It must be done at increments to keep the leader safe, and it must be done correctly, or there is no reason to do it at all. The clip has four steps: first, get a stance, then get the quickdraw and clip the bolt, then clip the rope, and then get moving! Seems simple, and yet a complex negotiation of some very specific risks must also happen in those steps. We commonly witness a high volume of errors around the skills of clipping. Whether it is a poor quickdraw attachment to the bolt, back clipping or Z-clipping the rope, missed clips/dropped rope when clipping, or inefficient technique, mistakes happen all the time during the vital process of clipping a quickdraw to a bolt and the rope into that quickdraw.

Four "Gets" of Sport Climbing Clipping

1. Get the stance

2. Get the quickdraw (orient correctly) and clip to bolt)

3. Get the rope (and correctly clip it into the quickdraw)

4. Get moving

A sport climber clipping.

The carabiner that clips to the rope must be the carabiner that routinely clips to the rope, and the carabiner that clips to the bolt must be the carabiner that routinely clips to the bolt. The repeated application of those carabiners to those two tasks (rope clipping and bolt clipping) unfortunately dedicates those carabiners to those tasks in perpetuity. Aluminum carabiners that clip to stainless steel bolt hangers tend to sustain tiny hanger-shaped scratches and nicks. When that bolt-clipping carabiner, scratched and nicked as it is, is then used to clip the rope, the scratches and nicks, when weighted or fallen upon, can have a devastating effect on the rope. Lead falls on the nicked carabiners can strip the sheath off of the rope or dangerously compromise the core integrity. So, bolt carabiners clip bolts. Rope carabiners clip ropes.

A locker draw places a locking carabiner in both sides of the textile. The locking mechanism on each carabiner provides security from gate interference, back clipping, and other bizarre occurrences. Forces from climber and rope motion can rotate/affect the position of your quickdraws. Having a couple locker draws for every lead can be a valuable precaution when weird things pop up on the lead. If the rabbit hole of hypotheticals has swallowed you whole, you can even go so far as to place locker draws on every single bolt, on every single lead. But you might be overmanaging just a little bit . . . or a lot!

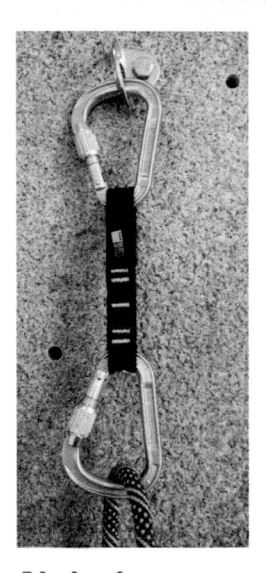

A locker draw.

The clipping process ideally occurs at about waist to chest height—not too high and not too low. This reality is a bit counterintuitive, and it flies in the face of the leader's instinct to clip the bolt as soon as possible, but it is an undisputed truth. If the leader reaches up to clip, slack must be pulled into the belay to reach up to that clip. If an unexpected fall happens at that moment, the extra distance (x2) will be added to the length of the lead fall. Whereas clipping at the waist does not introduce that slack in the first place.

Of course, while these ideal clipping positions are mathematically undisputed, mitigating factors could include the quality of the holds the climber can reach when the clip is at waist level. In other words, a leader should not hesitate to reach up to clip if that stance increases the likelihood of actually making the clip.

Clipping Commands

Leader: **"Clipping."** Quickdraw is attached to bolt. Leader is ready to clip the rope. Belayer needs to gives an appropriate amount of slack.

Belayer: Gives approximately two to three arm lengths of slack.

Leader: **"Clipped."** Leader has clipped rope into runner/quickdraw.

Belayer: Belays excessive slack out of the system.

Too often, however, leaders reach up to clip impulsively, because the looming lead fall is terrifying. The irony is that those long-reach clips are sometimes more strenuous and more dangerous, and they actually exacerbate the terror the leader is impulsively trying to subdue. You are at a greater risk if you fall while clipping. Stances on the rock may dictate other clipping heights, but try to work in the ergonomic, efficient, and risk-managing waist-high position. If you reach down low, you have passed by the bolt and have created a longer-distance fall potential. This low, potentially awkward movement can also jeopardize your stance. If you reach too high when clipping, you again can be forced into awkward and strenuous stances and must pull out extra rope. This increases the fall distance. Long fall potential and bad (awkward/strenuous) stances are not a good combo to clip from!

Quickdraw Clipping

Quickdraw length is a consideration. A longer quickdraw could help with issues like rope drag and

A clip gone awry. The nose of this notch-style carabiner is hung up on the bolt. Keyhole carabiners have a lower profile and are less likely to get fouled on a bolt. Always properly manage/attach the quickdraw to the bolt.

minimize negative carabiner gate–bolt hanger interactions. But the longer length will increase fall length.

Select a quickdraw. Do you have a need for a longer or shorter length? Longer lengths may straighten the rope path and minimize rope drag that wears at a climber and makes the climb feel even harder. Shorter quickdraws will minimize fall distance and can be more rigid and easy to clip. Do you want the security of a locker draw? In what orientation do you need the quickdraw to be? Generally the spine of the carabiner should be located in the anticipated direction of travel/fall. Are there any levering or carabiner integrity/loading issues? Clip the quickdraw into the bolt and move toward the rope.

Beware of quickdraw accessories (usually some sort of rubber band/fastener) that help stabilize/stiffen the rope-clipping carabiner to further facilitate easy clipping of the rope. These have been misused with tragic results. Ensure that carabiners are properly through the quickdraw's soft good textile material, not just the rubber stabilizer—it will not hold you! This more rigid end should be reserved for the carabiner that the rope is clipped into, both for easier clipping and because the carabiner connected to a hanger can develop burrs or sharp edges over time; if it is inadvertently switched to the end that the rope is clipped into, it could compromise/damage your rope. We advocate visual and tactile inspection of all climbing equipment prior to use!

Rope Clipping

It is now time to integrate the bolt protection component and your quickdraw attachment by clipping the rope into the lower carabiner of the quickdraw. This is the process that creates the most errors! Start with your hand at your tie-in knot, move your hand down the rope, communicate "clipping," pull up the rope, and use a comfortable method to clip the rope into the carabiner. Communicate "clipped." Examine for errors. Climb on.

There are numerous hand techniques to facilitate clipping the rope. Two common ones are outlined below. Many climbers use different techniques depending on which way the carabiner faces, which side of the body the carabiner is located on, and which hand is free to clip.

Finger method. Grab the rope between thumb and a finger(s) and stabilize the carabiner with a different finger while clipping the rope into the carabiner. The finger method usually involves stabilizing the carabiner with your middle finger and clipping the rope while it is held/pushed by the thumb and index finger. The middle finger serves as a stabilizing pivot point for clipping.

Clipping methods. Left side (top and bottom)—Big Pinches, Right Side (top and bottom)—Finger Methods

Big pinch method. Grab the rope between thumb and a finger or rest it in the notch between thumb and fingers. Pinch the whole carabiner while clipping the rope into the carabiner. The big pinch method commonly involves pinching the carabiner with the whole hand. The rope is clipped from a resting point at the base of the thumb or from between two fingers.

Practicing Clipping

Clipping is a skill that needs to be practiced. Any hanging carabiner and a rope (or section of rope) will allow you to practice. Practice the rope-clipping methods and how you apply them to the possible carabiner, body, and hand orientations.

Possible Orientations to Practice Clipping

- Left-facing gate, left body side, left hand

- Left-facing gate, left body side, right hand

- Left-facing gate, right body side, left hand

- Left-facing gate, right body side, right hand

- Right-facing gate, left body side, left hand

- Right-facing gate, left body side, right hand

- Right-facing gate, right body side, left hand

- Right-facing gate, right body side, right hand

Rope Clipping Errors

The errors possible when clipping the rope are back clipping and Z–clipping, and both have consequences. A back clip is when the rope is clipped so that it does not go up through the carabiner from bottom to top, but rather from top to bottom. This puts a twist in the rope, which could lead to the rope unclipping from the carabiner if it is fallen upon by the climber. Another way to think of this is that the rope is clipped in the wrong direction into a carabiner. Think of the carabiner as having a bottom (against the rock) and a top (facing out from the rock). The rope needs to go from bottom to top . . . just like a climber!

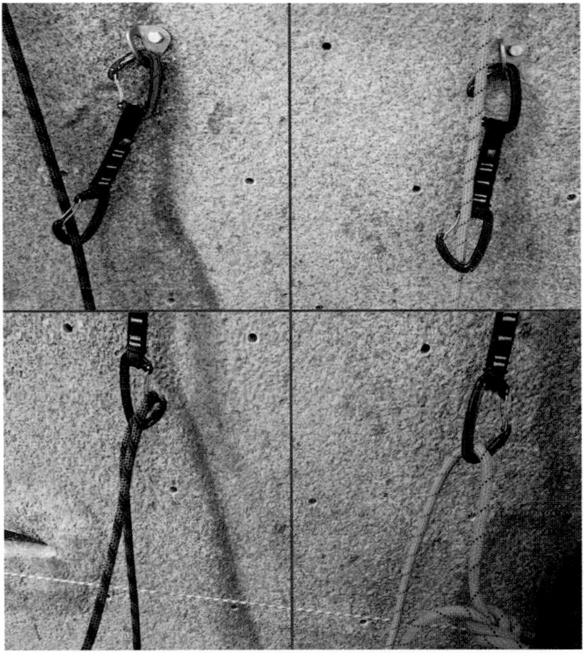

Examples of back clipping (left side, top and bottom) and proper clipping (right side, top and bottom).

A twisty attachment can hide a back clip. Straighten quickdraw attachments before clipping the rope!

Z-clipping occurs when the order of bolts clipped is out of sequence. Bolts should be clipped in order (first, second, third, etc.) and the rope should run in a straight line without back clips. If bolts are closely spaced together, the climber, if not careful, could grab the rope from below the last bolt (instead of above) and then clip it into the newly placed quickdraw. The results would be a Z configuration in the rope, tons of rope drag, and a longer fall potential than expected.

Z-clipping.

Clipping the Rope

1. Start with your hand at your tie-in knot.

2. Move your hand down the rope.

3. Communicate "clipping."

4. Pull up the rope.

5. Use a comfortable method to clip the rope into the carabiner.

6. Communicated "clipped."

7. Examine for errors.

8. Climb on.

What if you back clip? Stop your advance up the climb and return to the scene of the error. Leave the back-clipped quickdraw in place and attempt to leapfrog in a new and correct one. Once a properly clipped quickdraw is in place, you can clean the original incorrect one. If the clipping space on the bolt will not allow this, the back-clipped draw may need to be removed and reoriented correctly.

What if you Z-clip? Stop your advance up the climb and return to the scene of the error. Unclip the rope from the last quickdraw and reclip it in the correct manner.

The belayer is a watchful eye and risk manager for the climber and could help prevent these errors!

CHAPTER 6

Leading and Falling

The joys of sport climbing really arrive when all the other pieces are in place: the belay is secure, competent, and reliable; the research has been done;

Starting a sport climb under the protection of a stick clipped first bolt. Note the belayer's position, the neatly managed rope with the other rope end closed and protruding.

the challenges await; and each move and each clip summon forth all the skill and poise the climber can muster. This is the moment the climber has been waiting for. And yet, so many skills must be deployed during the lead to optimize enjoyment and allow the leader to focus on leading. Many leaders attempt to lead with an inchoate skill set, thinking, "I'll figure the rest out as I go."

Don't attempt to lead until all the prerequisite skills are ready.

Prerequisite Skills for Sport Climbing

A good sport climbing progression before attempting an actual lead:

1. Learn to toprope, and master all the skills that apply to that activity.
2. Work on movement and climbing technique! (This is not a movement technique text; there are plenty of great ones out there!)
3. Learn to lead belay. Catching lead falls, watching a lead climber move, and communicating with a lead climber are good ways to lay a foundation for leading.
4. Learn to clean the leads of others.
5. Learn to clip.
6. Learn to anchor.
7. Learn to fall.
8. Lead easy climbs.
9. Lead harder climbs and practice falling.

The Leading Process

The leading process has its own sort of repetitive rhythm. It flows through setup and double-checks, belaying, leading, and anchoring. When the climbing team starts to feel the rhythm of these events, it is easier to notice dysrhythmia and problems, and it becomes easier to avert accidents. The process:

- The first clip has been stick clipped or spotting up to it has occurred.

- The leader reaches each clip, selects an appropriate quickdraw, and clips the fixed protection bolt in a deliberate manner (see chapter 5).

- Climber: "Clipping." This alerts the belayer that the leader needs an amount of slack in order to clip the rope into the quickdraw.

- The belayer gives out an appropriate amount of slack.

- The leader clips the rope into the quickdraw, says, "Clipped," and continues.

A sport climber resting.

- This process repeats itself until the leader has reached the anchor. The leader avoids grabbing or stepping on bolts (or any fixed anchors). The belayer watches for back clips, Z-clips, and the rope running behind the climber's leg. Communication is common (e.g., "Clear the rope").

Falling Skills

Falling is a part of climbing, crucial to progressing in the sport and central to climbers continually challenging themselves. There is no subdiscipline of climbing that is more suited to falling than sport climbing. Sport climbing's essence is to focus on climbing movement in terrain that is equipped to minimize risk. With that said, hazards are present and there is an effective or proper way to fall. Even when these falling methods are employed, numerous conditions can be present that make the risk and consequences real. Philosophically, some prefer not to focus on falling and are reluctant to constantly assess the consequences of a fall throughout a climb. We advocate this constant assessment process and practice at falling.

How to Fall

There are numerous components to proper falling. First, get an experienced and effective belayer. He/she will not only employ proper belay techniques but will also serve as another set of eyes to help identify and manage hazards. Second, identify hazards in the landing areas. The route should be previewed in person and in guidebooks. Look down and assess when climbing. Are there blocks or ledges you would not want to hit? A sound practice is to look at where you want to land

*A climber falling in the force-absorbing cat position—
Rrrr!*

when falling—a nice clean area. The body tends to
follow the focus of the eyes. Third, communicate with
your belayer. Use "Watch me" when a fall is looking imminent and "Falling" when a fall occurs. These
commands are great to help your belayer perform his/
her role! Fourth, relax and become a falling cat. Legs
and arms should be bent and "loose"—ready to be
shock absorbers in the muscles and joints. Hands are
out and do not grab/snag on the rope, quickdraws, or
rock. Breathe and give a good yell/cat roar. Don't push

Falling Tips

- Have a good belayer.

- Be aware of hazards in the landing area.

- Communicate—use the commands "Watch me" and "Falling."

- Become a falling cat. Relax—breathe and become a shock absorber.

- Bend your legs and arms and have your hands out.

- Don't push off.

- Ensure that your legs hit the rock first.

off; this can increase the force with which you slam into the rock. Legs should hit first and start the force-absorbing process.

Falling

There are many cases where a fall is not ideal, is high risk, and may not be central to the climber's well-being and progression in sport climbing. This is the case when a climber cannot become a falling cat shock absorber and will hit something hard. Low-angle rock, landing zones with ledges, blocks, flakes, and belayers are all hard. Hitting them will be unpleasant. You can avoid routes of this nature or ensure that they are well within your abilities. You should be aware of the route's characteristics and make informed decisions. Belayers and climbers can work together to ensure that they do not crash into each other during a

Clear the rope. This climber will be rope burned and likely flipped over if a fall occurs.

fall. Stick clipping, spotting, and belay stances are great avoidance tools. Keeping the rope path clear of the climber's body is crucial. If the rope is not clear and behind a leg, a fall could yield rope burns at a minimum or complete inversion and a head-first fall (along with the rope burns) as a strong possibility. A rope that is clear is one that is in front of the climber's body and positioned with the direction of movement in mind. If this direction is straight up, the rope should be in front of the body and straight up between the legs. If the climbing direction is to the left, the rope should be in front and coming off the right hip. If the climbing direction is to the right, the rope should be in front and coming off the left hip. Falling when a clipping error has occurred is another hazard to avoid.

Falling Practice

With a desire to get better at falling, a knowledge of how to fall, a knowledge of falling hazards, and some basic physics, falling practice can be set up and managed. As with any skill, you will get better at falling if you practice, which in turn may alleviate your fears when climbing.

Set yourself up to succeed when practicing. Choose terrain that is slightly overhanging and somewhat long. The practice should occur far up the climb, where you can utilize the dynamic properties of every climber's most important tool: the rope. Start at this high point of the climb, falling on a "mini toprope" under the clipped quickdraw. Now move to being even with the quickdraw and fall. Repeat and gradually move up, leaving the security of the mini toprope/proximity to the quickdraw and start taking small lead falls: 1 foot above quickdraw, 2 feet above quickdraw, etc. Progress with good falling technique and ensure that you constantly assess the hazards as the terrain and fall paths change. Some climbers use a locked locker draw to enhance security for this falling practice.

CHAPTER 7

Anchoring

In sport climbing, anchoring at the top of a climb is actually part of leading. It is a skill that the leader cannot do without, and yet because the anchor tends to punctuate the leading, it is often treated as an afterthought. It should not be. If a lead climber has spent time toproping (as he/she should), the anchoring challenges in sport climbing should seem discrete and straightforward. We've already mentioned in previous chapters how the hardware on the cliff tends to be more uniform and standardized in sport climbing. There are only three fixed anchor styles/configurations: small opening, large opening, and quick/direct. All three have two strong component bolts. As a result, anchoring is a much more standardized practice as well.

In this chapter we will review the principles that govern all anchor building, sport climbing anchors included. We will explore the handful of circumstances that might dictate what kind of anchor to build. The variables are fairly predictable: There are a few different kinds of anchoring bolts, the anchors could be loaded in a few different ways, and there may be some toproping after the lead (or none at all).

Fundamental Anchoring Principles

Sport climbing anchors should strive to apply the same fundamental principles as toprope anchors, namely NERDSS. A sport climbing anchor is

NERDSS

No Extension: If an unexpected failure of any part of the anchor system occurs, the master point should not extend/minimally extend. This avoids shock loading the remaining anchor parts or dropping a climber an unacceptable distance.

Redundancy: Imagine the failure of any component or segment. Are there other components, attachments, or master point construction to back it up and ensure redundancy?

Distribution: An anchor system and its master point should be perfectly positioned on the desired climb so that when the largest loads are applied to it, the attachment system distributes loads (shares) to the components as intended and there is no multiplying of forces. Do you need a unidirectional or multidirectional sharing? Location, sharing, and angle are the distribution factors to be examined.

Strength: An anchor should be strong enough to hold all potential loads that the climbing team can generate.

Simplicity: The anchor should be timely and simple.

Speed? For sport climbing, an extra *S* for Speed may be a valid emphasis, as sport climbing anchors are typically on a cliff face with poor stances. A build will initially occur at the end of a sport lead when first constructed, when the climber might be tired. It is also great to spend your day climbing and not anchoring!

gcncrally more straightforward, however, because the anchor bolts tend to suggest a handful of consistently applied rigging techniques.

With respect to the fundamental principles of anchoring, there are four primary anchoring configurations sport climbers will need to rely on: a two-quickdraw anchor, a locker draw anchor, a unidirectional anchor like the ponytail (with a 4-foot sling or cordellette), and a multidirectional anchor like the quad (with a 4-foot sling or cordellette). Certain contexts and circumstances suggest the application of one technique or another. There are other configurations (see photo on page 100) that may be useful for sport climbing or for sport climbers desiring to move into traditional climbing. The four primary options are not arbitrary. Instead, a sport climber will need to understand the subtle advantages and disadvantages of each technique. All these anchoring configurations will work on any of the three fixed anchor styles. The first question becomes what are you going to use a fixed anchor for? The next questions center around how will it become loaded with force, by whom, from what directions, and for how long.

Uses of Sport Climbing Anchors

This is a pretty obvious list on the surface (in order of frequency!):

- Lowering
- Toproping
- Rappelling

Here's the ideal case—the way sport climbing anchors should be:

Quick/direct anchors are simple and do not require any further equipment from the leader, unless toproping is going to occur by others in the climbing team. This fixed-anchor style is the ultimate standard. Upon arrival at the anchor, the rope clips directly into these two components, and the leader proceeds to be lowered to the ground. Rappelling does not make sense when lowering is so easy. Typically, the quickdraws used along the way by the leader would be removed from the pitch as the leader lowers. Quick/direct anchors have been installed to facilitate these kinds of quick exchanges and minimalism at the anchor, but their generosity should not be abused. They are there for leading, and toprope parties should either build their own anchor (see methods below) or find another climb.

Four Primary Sport Climbing Anchor Configurations

Two-quickdraw anchor. A generation ago, the two-quickdraw anchor quickly became the iconic sport climbing anchor. But the context of that anchor should not be forgotten. Those climbing parties rarely toproped. One climber led the pitch, and the next climber pulled the rope, led the pitch, and then cleaned. So, the climbing team was almost never exposed to the two quickdraws as the sole protection, because all the other quickdraws were clipped in when the leader lowered. When modern climbers find themselves back in this context, the two-quickdraw anchor can be deployed satisfactorily.

Anchoring Method	Ideal Application	Poor Application
Two-quickdraw anchor	• When the leader intends to pull the rope so the second climber can lead.	• Toproping • When the anchor location and quickdraw length do not yield a load-sharing anchor. All the force is on one draw.
Locker draw anchor	• When the fall line-direction of loading is directly underneath the anchor and the second climber intends to toprope.	• When the direction of load for the toprope varies. • When the anchor location and locker draw length do not yield a load-sharing anchor. All the force is on one draw.
Traditional two-piece anchor—unidirectional load sharing (Pony Tail, Cool X, atomic clip [bunny-eared figure 8])	• When multiple climbers hope to toprope a climb after the lead, and the direction of loading is directly underneath the anchor.	• When the direction of load for the toprope varies. • In a small team (two climbers), or when more than one climber is not planning to toprope.
Self-adjusting anchor—multidirectional load sharing (Quad, magic X, equalette, multidirectional atomic clip [bunny-eared figure 8])	• When multiple climbers hope to toprope a climb after the lead, and the direction of loading varies due to climbers' path or clipping and unclipping directionals	• When adding time and materials to create these more complex rigs is consequential and burdensome. Note: Some can be pre-rigged (Quad)

The classic two-quickdraw anchor approach to sport climbing.

Two–locker draw anchor. Many climbers do not find the two-quickdraw anchor to be very encouraging once the rest of the quickdraws on the pitch are unclipped. Indeed, it can be unnerving to toprope 100 feet up to an anchor and see two plain nonlocking carabiners protecting life and limb. Locker draws are a much more reassuring sight. A pair of them, opposite and opposed, creates a much more secure connection at each bolt and the toprope.

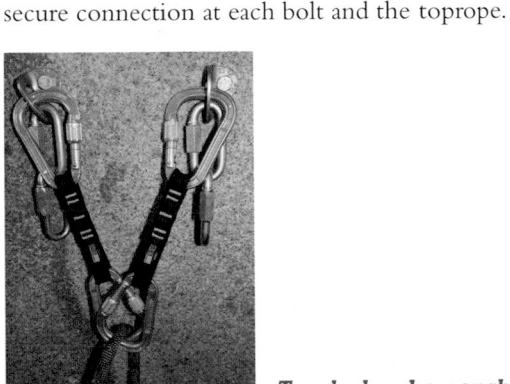

Two-locker draw anchor.

Traditional unidirectional load sharing two-component anchor—the Pony Tail. For protracted sessions of toproping after a sport lead, the traditional unidirectional anchor best adheres to the fundamental principles of anchoring as we know them. It creates adequate strength, has material redundancy throughout its construction, distributes load to the bolts in a compelling way, and is fairly simple. This method relies on forces being applied in one direction. The anchor loses its effectiveness if the direction of pull/load on it changes.

Traditional multidirectional load-sharing two-component anchor—the Quad. Again, when protracted sessions of toprope follow a sport lead and the removal of quickdraws changes the way the anchor is loaded. There are multiple directions of load possible by a falling toproper that are not directionalized by quickdraws or the Pony Tail anchor. A traditional self-adjusting multi-directional anchor like the Quad best adheres to the fundamental principles of anchoring as we know them. It creates adequate strength, has material redundancy throughout its construction, distributes load to the bolts in a compelling way, and is fairly simple. This method does NOT rely on forces only being applied in one direction. This anchor does not lose its effectiveness if the direction of pull/load on it changes over its self-adjusting range.

Why so many ways to anchor? Having an understanding of the riggings above gives a builder choice and a skill set to build with multiple attachment materials. The materials at hand really should not matter; a NERDSS anchor can be built regardless, and a forgotten attachment material or unfamiliar set of circumstances should not cause a spike in risk or slow down your climbing day.

Composite photos of some less common anchor building options. L to R, top to bottom: atomic clip (bunny-eared figure 8) and sling with magic X and limiting knots, two slings with magic Xs, and the Cool X (a knotted sling clipped on either side). These options are used to varying degrees. The four primary anchor configurations are most common, especially the Pony Tail and the Quad. It is important to know multiple anchor rigging methods utilizing multiple materials, so you can anchor in any situation and climb on!

Common Anchor Choices in Detail

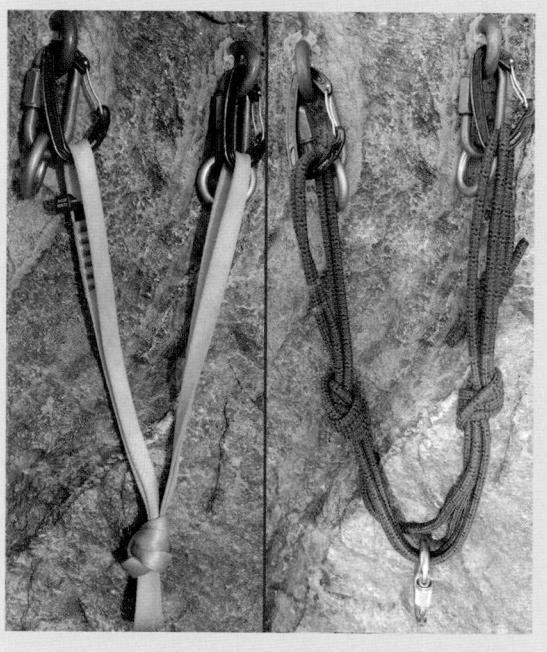

Left: Pony Tail anchor.   *Right: Quad anchor.*

Pony Tail anchor.

Component: two bolts.

Attachment: runner.

Master point: overhand on a bight.

Evaluation via NERDSS

  No extension: Yes

  Redundancy: All but the climbing rope.

Runner is rigged to be redundant as an attachment and at the master point

Distribution: Runner rigging shares the load unidirectionally

Strength: Strong bolts, rope, runner, and carabiners

Simplicity: Very efficient and timely

Speed: Not as fast as locker draws—Another unidirectional configuration

Quad anchor.

Component: two bolts.

Attachment: cordellette rigged into Quad configuration.

Master point: 3 of 4 Quad pocket strands.

Evaluation via NERDSS

No extension: Yes, minimal

Redundancy: All but the climbing rope. Cordellette is rigged to be redundant as an attachment and at the master point

Distribution: Cordellette rigging shares the load multidirectionally

Strength: Strong bolts, rope, cordellette, and carabiners

Simplicity: Very efficient and timely

Speed: If prerigged, as fast as clipping

An anchor builder should run through this evaluation progression with NERDSS after building an anchor.

Anchoring Sequences

Frustratingly, anchoring is the last thing a lead climber must accomplish before finally resting on the rope and lowering to the group. Given the time and energy it takes to complete, this final chore unfortunately has been the scene of many blunders, miscommunications, and incidents. It need not be.

Setting up a toprope anchor.

This essential process is the same for small-opening, large-opening, and quick/direct fixed anchor styles.

- Remain on belay throughout this process. Approach the fixed anchor and put one quickdraw into one of the anchor's bolt components and clip the rope into it (or clip the rope immediately into the quick/direct-style component). While protected by this clip and your continuing belay, rig an anchor of choice and clip the rope through the master point carabiners.

- Unclip the rope from the quickdraw (or quick/direct component) and remove it from the fixed anchor.

- Communicate and have the belayer take slack and tighten you.

- Communicate and have the belayer lower you.

- The toprope is ready to go!

Other commands tend to give belayers the impression that their services are no longer required. But of course they are. Stay on belay!

If there is not an adequate stance at the anchor bolts for rigging, clip the anchor and call for tension. Even if there is a stance, manage risk immediately when arriving at an anchor; create a mini toprope with a quickdraw and the rope, to protect your anchor-rigging process!

Immediate lower with quick/direct clips.

- Remain on belay throughout this process.

- Clip the rope into each anchor component.

- Communicate and have the belayer take slack and tighten you.

- Communicate and have the belayer lower you.

CHAPTER 8

Cleaning

Much like a child who must clean up toys after playing with them, someone will need to clean up a sport climb. The quickdraws must be removed, the anchor must be removed, and the climber/cleaner will want to be safe and efficient in the process. We again mention these two values because they are supposed to work in concert with one another. Many climbers manage to stay safe when cleaning an anchor, but the sequence they use is overwrought, is overly complex, and requires a small arsenal of extra equipment. Incidentally, the unnecessary complications of the cleaning sequences can be the source of their own hazards, either when new climbers are attempting to emulate those sequences or when experienced climbers are distracted.

The cleaning sequences recommended in this text have some fundamental assumptions that may seem controversial at first.

- We assume that a **dynamic belay system** is the most effective system for keeping a climber safe, when leading, when cleaning, and when descending. We will therefore advocate for an unremitting reliance on that system.

- We assume that one **lowering** climber **does not** have a severe impact on the longevity of an anchor's master/focal point(s). We accept that rappelling sequences have less impact on rappel rings, but the value of a rappelling sequence is largely overshadowed by an opportunity to be safer and more efficient through lowering. In short, we think it's worth it to replace rap rings more often as a result of lowering, for the sake of safety and efficiency.

- We assume that cleaning sequences that do not require any additional equipment (like when utilizing quick/direct style fixed anchors), or ones that require only **minimal equipment**, are valuable and constitute their own kind of efficiency.

The accident rates at sport crags suggest that concerted values of safety and efficiency need to be emphasized when sport climbers learn to clean their anchors. The number of incidents involving rappelling suggest that many are overestimating the value of rap rings compared to lives and limbs, how quickly lowering destroys those rings, and the actual utility of rappelling. Sometimes rappelling is the best choice to make when cleaning, but a dogmatic adherence to that sequence is probably not the answer.

Keeping your dynamic belay and putting minimal wear on an anchor for a single lower is the method advocated here!

The Ideal Cleaning Scenario: Quick/Direct Fixed Anchors

Our discussion throughout this text has led to favoring this style of anchor. Its utility, essence to the definition of sport climbing, and efficiency are some of the reasons why. Compare the cleaning sequence here with those of the fixed anchor styles below and decide for yourself!

- **Step 1 Stay on belay:** Upon reaching the anchor. Remain on belay throughout this process.

- **Step 2 Clip:** Clip the rope into each anchor quick/direct clip component.

- **Step 3 Communicate:** Communicate and have the belayer take you tight.

- **Step 4 Clean the anchor**, and **lower**

Connecting Yourself to an Anchor

As you will see, there are numerous methods for effectively connecting to an anchor. Realize that this is an important connection and that there are consequences if it is not secure. Nothing should be allowed to compromise this connection.

There are many ways to connect yourself to an anchor!

Ways to Connect to an Anchor at the Top of a Sport Climb

Nylon sling/daisy link (PAS)

- Girth hitch to both pieces of your harness (soft good path that mirrors the belay loop. Do not girth hitch to/on the belay loop).

- Clip to the anchor's master point with a locking carabiner.

Two quickdraws/one or two locker draws

- Clip one end of each to master point or protection component.

- Clip other end to belay loop in an opposite-and-opposed gate configuration.

Hybrid—quickdraw and daisy link

- Clip daisy link with locker into one component and a quickdraw into the other.

- Connect the quickdraw to a lower link in the daisy link.

- Add security to this connection with another carabiner.

Single strand of climbing rope

- Clove hitch above your tie-in knot and clip to the anchor's master point with a locking carabiner.

Stay tight/secure/underneath on whatever connection you use.

Cleaning Scenario 1: Large-Opening Fixed Anchors

The vast majority of the time, the following cleaning sequence is the safest and most efficient. It does not require the climber to relinquish the belay. It does not invite unnecessary or confusing communication.

Step 1: Connect. Upon arriving at the anchor, connect to its master point via an acceptable method. The idea is to continue to rely on the belay for ultimate security and work without maintaining a stance or a grip on the rock. Double-check to make sure the connection is secure and the carabiner is locked.

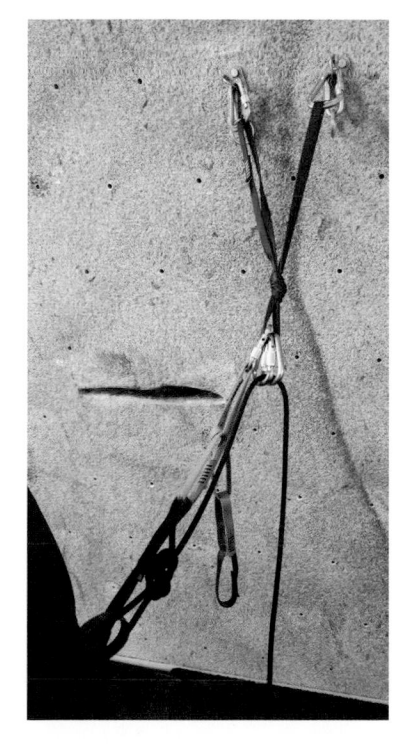

Cleaning scenario 1: large-opening anchor sequence.

Step 2: Thread a bight through the rap ring(s).

Call for slack, enough to run a bight of rope through the rap ring(s). Once the bight has been passed through the ring, a figure 8 on a bight should be tied.

Try to imagine the precision in this moment. The bight is now blocked against the rings. If anything were to go wrong, the climber is also secured by that blocked knot. The belayer did not hear anything confusing or distracting like "Off belay" or "In direct" or any other command that could suggest that relinquishing the belay is the next step.

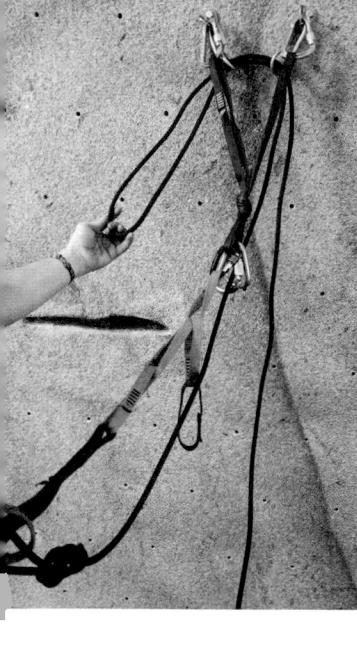
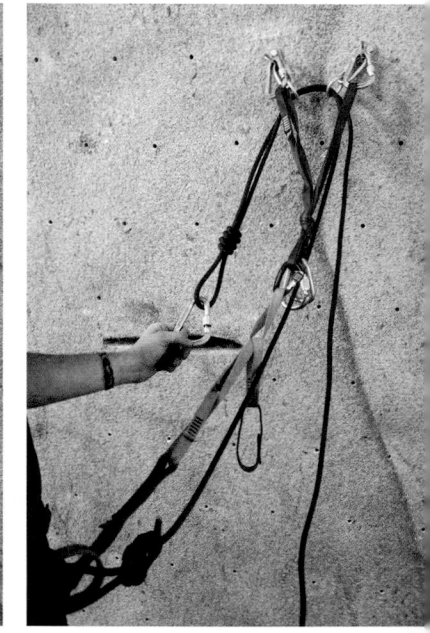

Step 3: Clip the figure 8 on a bight to the belay loop with a locking carabiner or two nonlocking carabiners (opposite and opposed). Once that bight knot is connected to the climber's belay loop, the climber may call to the belayer for tension or take. The belay will do so and be on a tight belay via the clipped-in bight.

Try to imagine the precision of this moment. Even if the belayer somehow misunderstood his/her role in the cleaning sequence, the call to take gives the climber a chance to feel tension and double-check the entire system before initiating any other critical steps. The climber is essentially anchored at this point by both the initial connection and the bight clipped to the belay loop and the original tie-in, which still has not been touched.

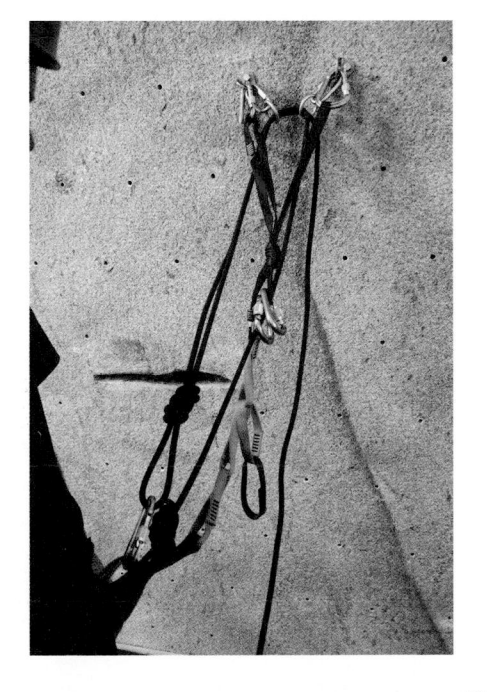

Step 4: Untie the original tie-in, clean the anchor, and lower. After double-checking all the critical links in the system (the belay/belayer, the bight knot, the locking carabiners, and the rope running through the rap rings), the climber can untie his/her original figure 8 follow through. That long tail can be pulled through the rings and allowed to dangle harmlessly behind the cleaner. The anchoring connection and materials can all be removed from the bolts and stowed. The climber can announce that he/she is ready to lower and allow the belayer to lower him/her to the ground.

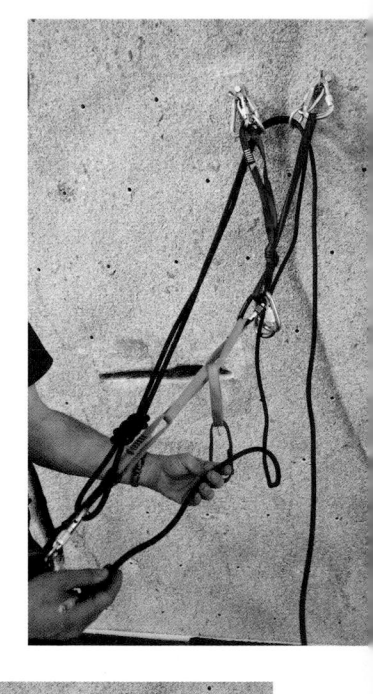

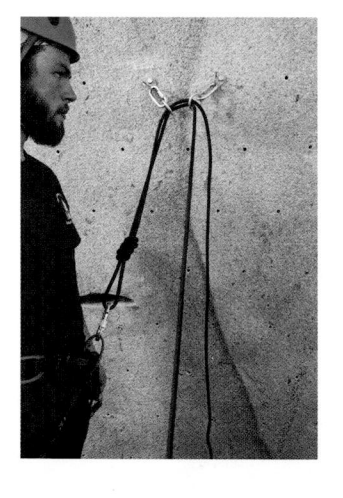

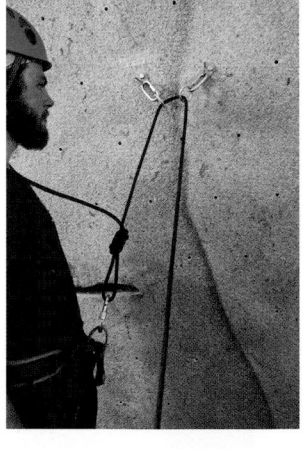

The cleaner never relinquished the belay. The cleaner was never untied from the rope and therefore did not create an opportunity to drop it. The cleaner communicated only three unambiguous commands to the belayer: "Slack," "Take," and "Ready to lower."

Connect to anchor.

▼

Call for "Slack."

▼

Use the slack to pass a bight of rope through the rap rings.

▼

Use the bight to tie a figure 8 on a bight.

▼

Attach the figure 8 on a bight to the belay loop with a locking carabiner or two nonlocking carabiners (opposite and opposed).

▼

Call "Take," and wait until the belayer does so.

▼

Double-check all critical links.

▼

Untie the original figure 8 follow through and pull the tail through the anchor.

▼

Disconnect from the anchor, and clean the anchoring materials.

▼

Call "Ready to lower" and lower.

Cleaning Scenario 2: Small-Opening Fixed Anchors

We will have to discuss this scenario, but it is becoming increasingly rare. The vast majority of sport climbing anchors are either quick/direct clips or large-opening style. The few remaining anchors that rely on small opening chain lengths probably also don't meet our criteria for a sport climb. But there is some overlap, so we will explore an alternative sequence for those sport climbs that still have small chain links at the anchor. It is easy to be resentful of those anchors, because the cleaning sequence they necessitate has none of the signature efficiency or elegance of the previous sequence. Maybe those chains can be systematically replaced as climbers grow to prefer a safer and more efficient cleaning sequence.

Step 1: Connect. Upon arriving at the anchor, connect to its master point via an acceptable method, and work without maintaining a stance or a grip on the rock. Double-check to make sure the connection is secure and the carabiner is locked.

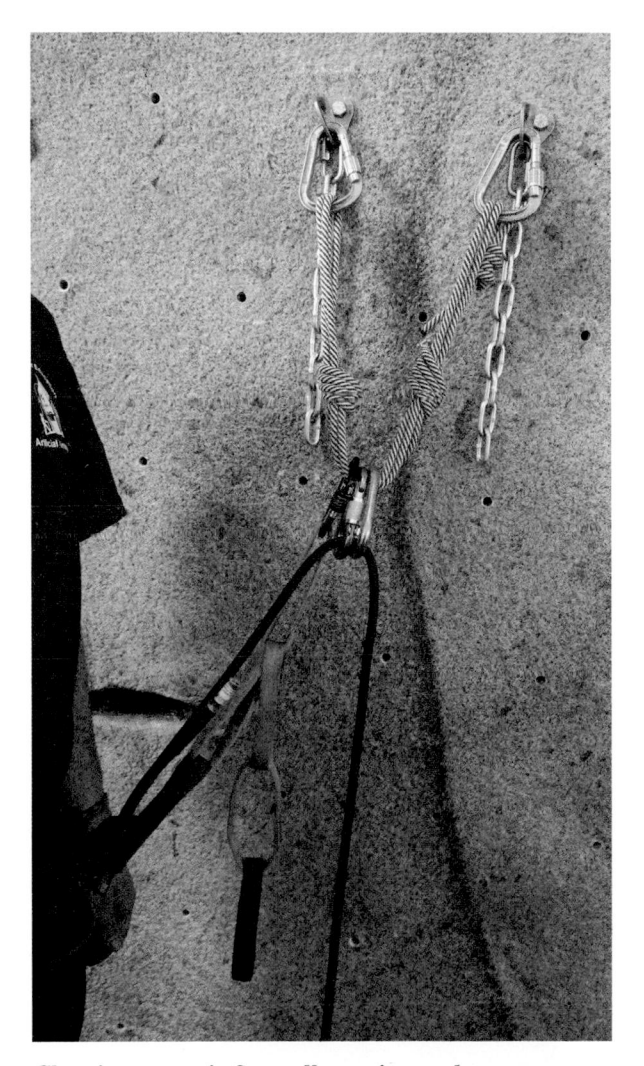

Cleaning scenario 2: small-opening anchor sequence.

Step 2: Secure the rope. Once tethered to the master point and double-checked, call "Slack." Pull up slack to tie a figure 8 on a bight and connect the bight knot to the belay loop with a locking carabiner. This connection secures the rope because the original figure 8 follow through will be untied in the next step. The rope cannot be dropped with this sequence!

Step 3a and b: Untie the original figure 8 follow through, pass through anchor, and retie.

Untie, then run the empty tail through the small chain links. Tie back in with a figure 8 follow through.

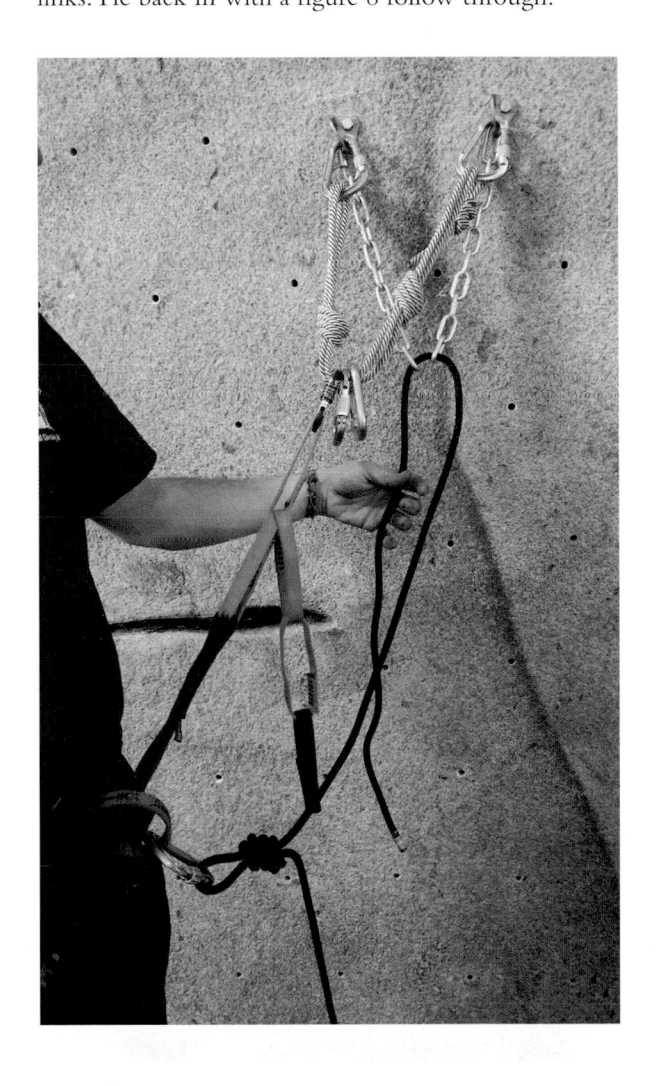

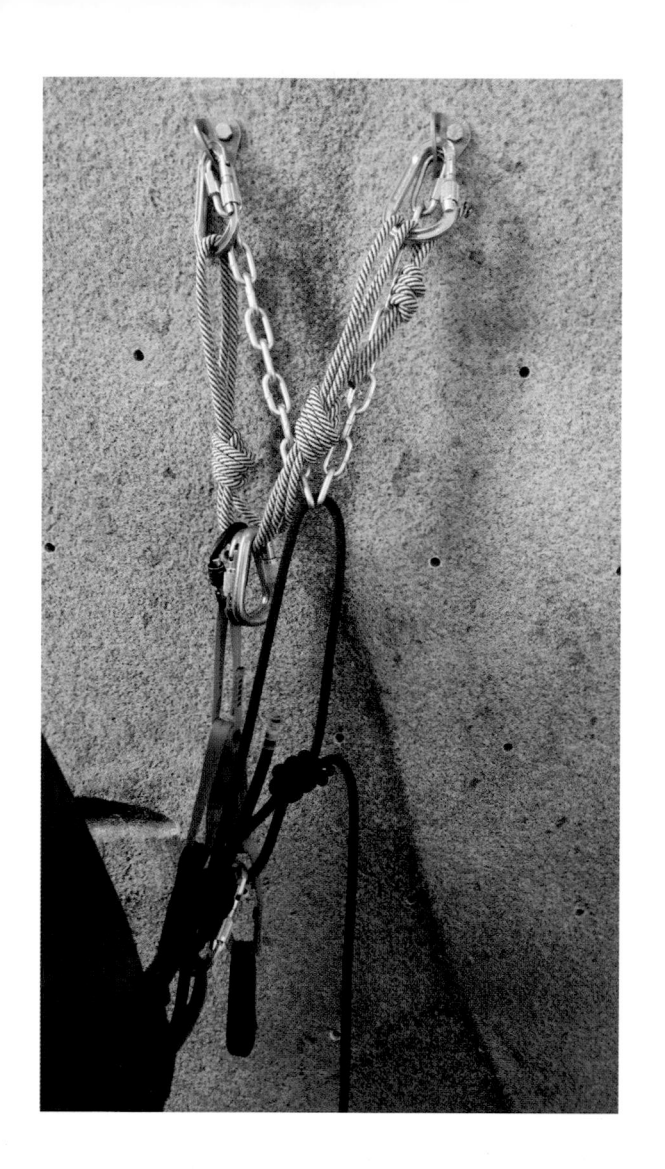

Step 4: Detach and untie the figure 8 on a bight. Detach and untie the placeholding figure 8 on a bight that was connected to the belay loop and call "Take" to the belayer.

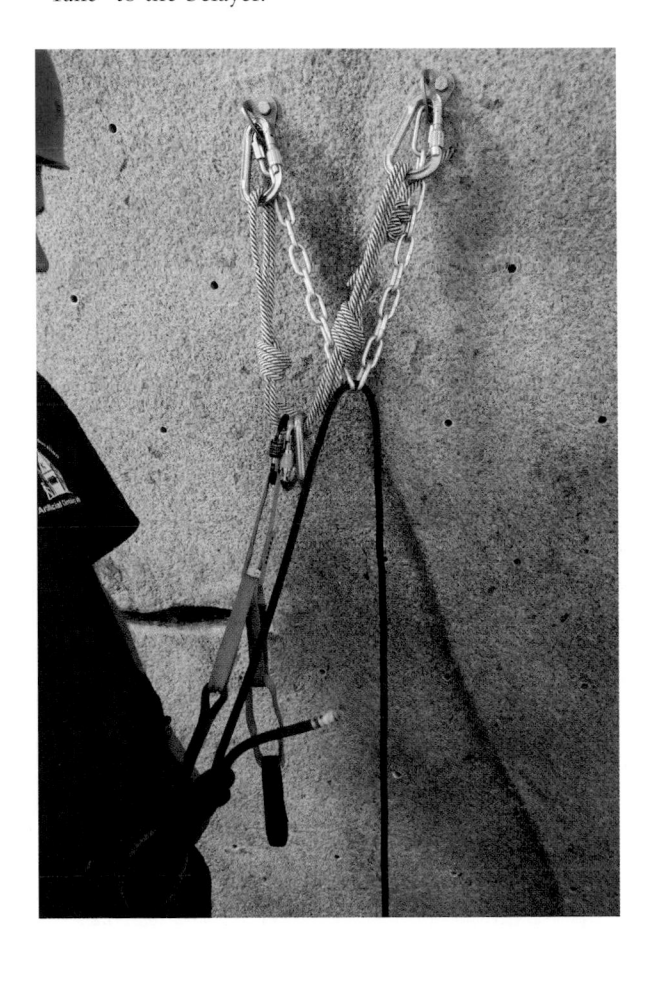

Step 5: Double-check all critical links, detach personal tether from anchor, clean anchor, and lower. Before detaching the personal tether and cleaning the anchor, perform a system check. Then call to the belayer, "Ready to lower."

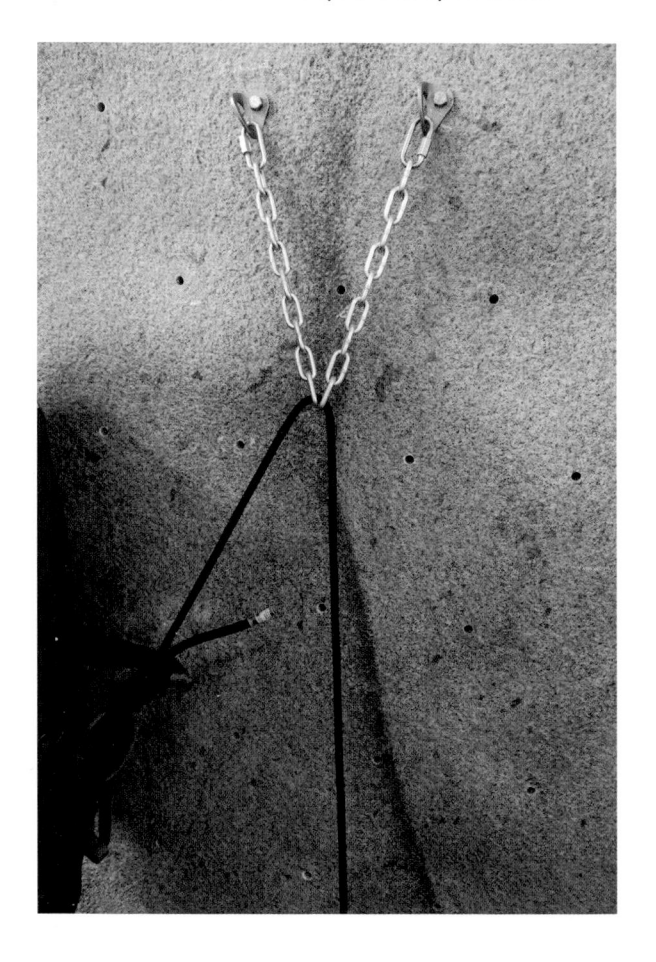

While this sequence is more cumbersome and requires more tools and steps than the previous sequence, it nevertheless avoids any ambiguous and confusing communication with the belayer. The climber announces "Slack," "Take," and "Ready to lower."

Connect to anchor.

▼

Call "Slack."

▼

Pull in two arm lengths of slack. Tie a figure 8 on a bight. Connect it to the belay loop with a locking carabiner

▼

Untie the original figure 8 follow through. Run it through the anchor's small openings. Tie back in with a figure 8 follow through.

▼

Detach and untie the figure 8 on a bight. Call "Take" to the belayer.

▼

1. Double-check all critical links.
2. Disconnect from anchor and clean the anchoring materials.

▼

Call "Ready to lower," and allow the belayer to lower.

Scenario 3: Cleaning by Rappelling

Some sport climbing cliffs are privately owned and there is a nonnegotiable expectation that climbers clean anchors by rappelling here and elsewhere. While these expectations arguably value rap rings more than lives and limbs, it is reasonable for a private landowner to establish nonnegotiable norms on his/her own property. So, all climbers should entitle these landowners to their norms. There are other scenarios where a sport climber may need to clean an anchor and rappel. Having rappelling in the toolbox is a smart cleaning sequence for these scenarios. Cleaning by rappelling is the only cleaning sequence that will relinquish the belay; therefore the plan to rappel, when that plan is justifiable, should be clearly communicated to the belayer before the climb or cleaning begins.

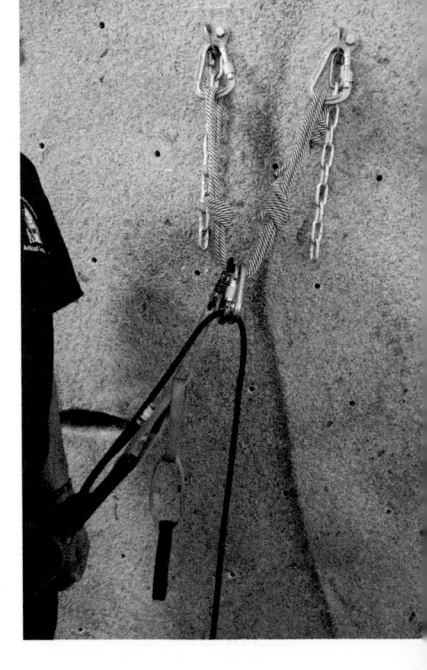

Step 1: Connect. Upon arriving at the anchor, connect to its master point via an acceptable method, and work without maintaining a stance or a grip on the rock. Double-check to make sure the connection is secure and the carabiner is locked.

Step 2: Call "Off belay." Communicate with the belayer and await a response.

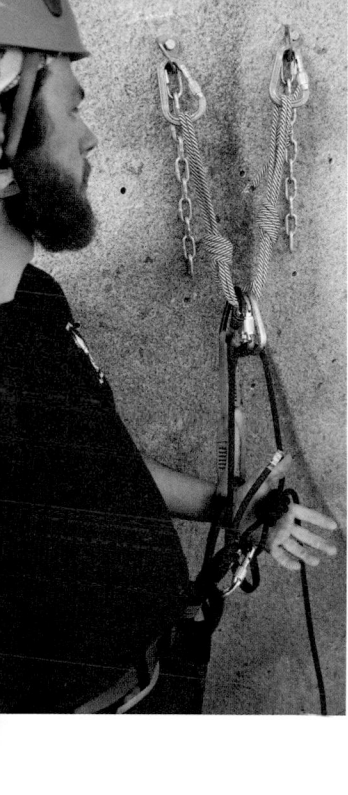

Step 3: Secure the rope.
Once tethered to the master point and double-checked, call "Slack." Pull up slack to tie a figure 8 on a bight and connect the bight knot to the belay loop with a locking carabiner. The rope cannot be dropped with this sequence!

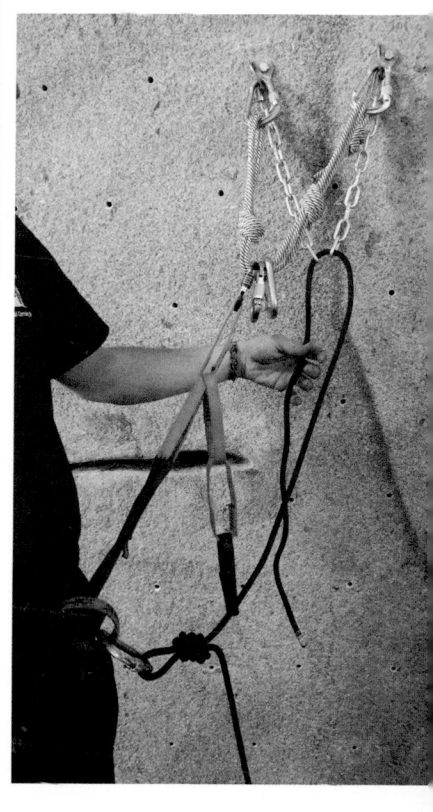

Step 4a and b: Untie the original figure 8 follow through, pass through anchor, and tie a stopper knot.
Thread the tail through the rap rings or chain links,

and tie a bulky stopper knot. The overhand on a bight is a good one. This knot will stop the rope from falling back through the rings and will close one end of the system, so be sure that it is bulky and tight.

Step 5: Detach and untie the figure 8 on a bight. Detach and untie the rope securing figure 8 on a bight that was connected to the belay loop.

Step 6: Pull the rope through the rings. Pull until the middle of the rope is at the anchor and both ends of the rope are on the ground with system-closing knots in each end.

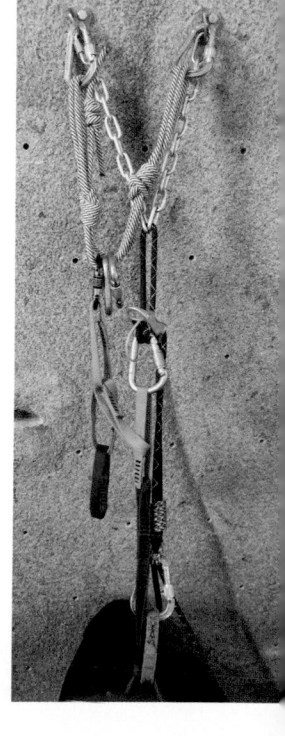

Step 7: Rig for rappel. Using an MBD (plate/aperture/tube device), set up both strands of rope in adjacent slots on the belay device. Connect and extend the belay device with a locking carabiner to the personal tether.

Step 8: Tie a friction hitch backup. Tie a backup, like an autoblock, around the two brake strands, and connect the hitch to the belay loop with a locking carabiner.

Step 9: Double-check all critical links. Make sure carabiners are locked, rappel is rigged correctly, middle of rope passes through rappel rings, and rope ends are on the ground with system-closing knots in each end.

Step 10: Detach personal tether from the anchor. Clean anchor. Rappel.

The reader should understand and intuit that the rappelling cleaning sequence puts the cleaner in a position all alone, at the anchor, with no belay system as a backup. So, it is a sequence that is replete with opportunities for error. It is a sequence that should

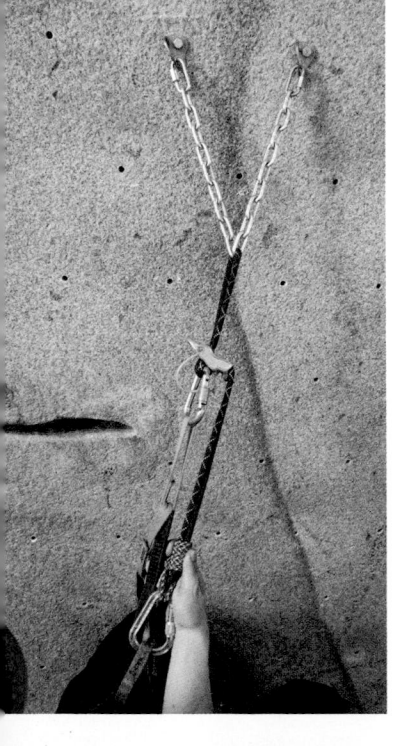

be practiced on the ground and thoroughly understood before being undertaken. Most of all, it is a technique whose clear applications are so rare, it is probably best reserved for those occasions where it is absolutely necessary. Sport climbers will hopefully applaud the day when it is finally extinct from the discipline.

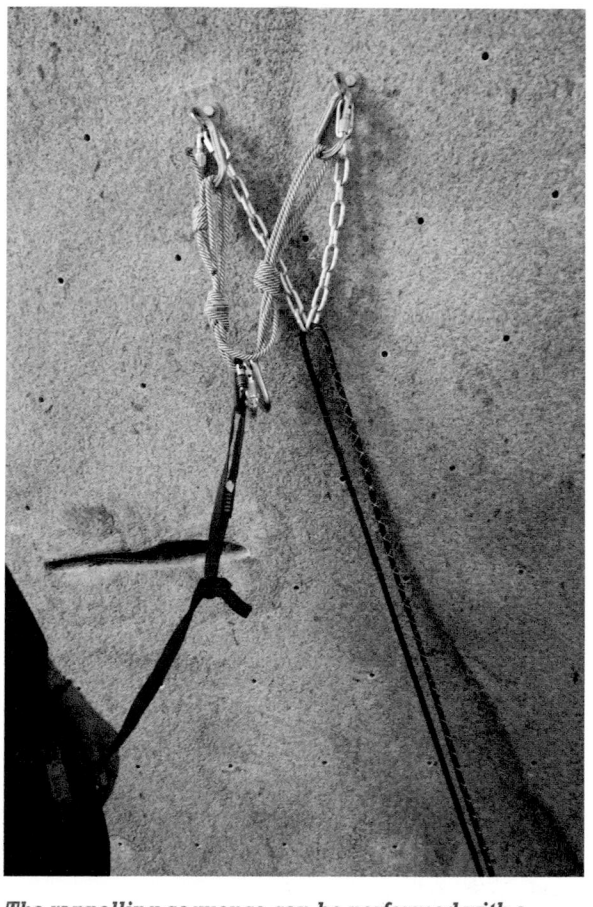

The rappelling sequence can be performed with a variety of personal tethers. In this example, a double-length sling girth hitched to the harness and with an overhand on bight knot is employed.

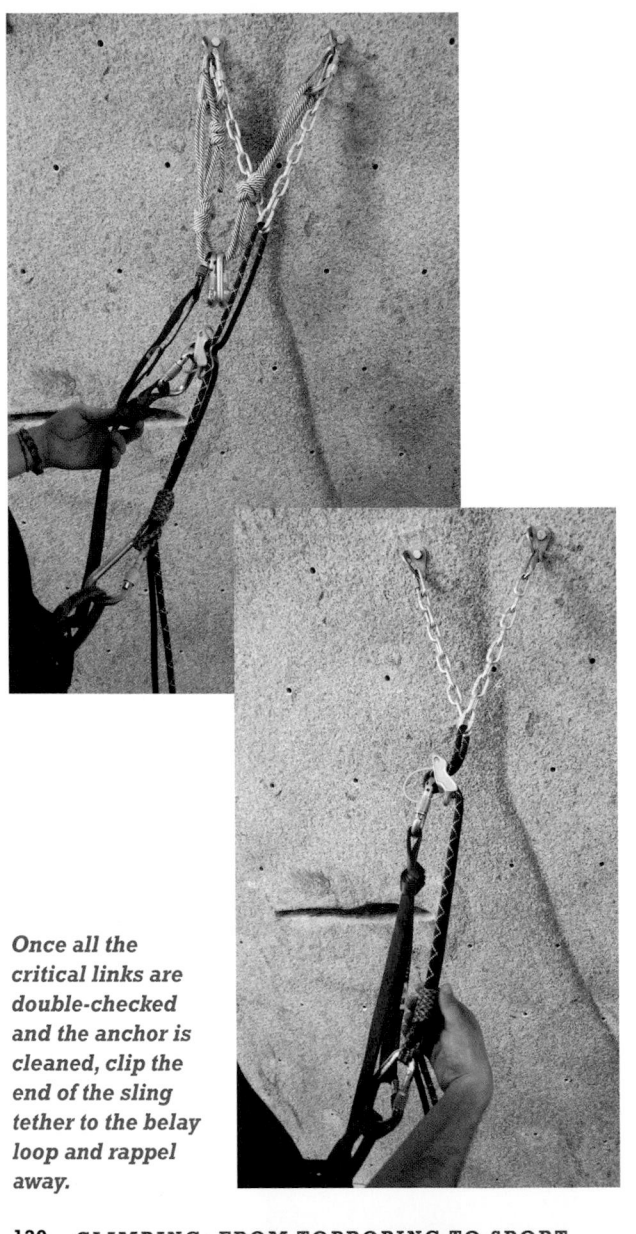

Once all the critical links are double-checked and the anchor is cleaned, clip the end of the sling tether to the belay loop and rappel away.

A fixed anchor rappel with an ABD. This blocked single-rope strand rappel also minimizes wear on the anchor. This rappelling alternative can be substituted for the extended autoblock rappell methods outlined earlier.

Remember: Regardless of the fixed anchor type, communicate the rappelling plan in advance, close the system, and ensure that your rope is managed correctly with the middle where it should be and both ends on the ground with knots in the ends.

Sport Climbing Shenanigans and Emergency Preparedness

Shenanigans for Clipping the First Bolt

Since clipping the first bolt is vital to prevent groundfall, sport climbing is full of crafty techniques for doing so. We will explore the most common techniques: the cheerleader technique, the improvised stick clip, and the manufactured stick clip.

The cheerleader technique. This technique is just as low-tech as it sounds. The lightest of two climbers ties in to the end of the rope; clips the climbing rope into a quickdraw, careful not to back clip; and climbs on his/her partner's shoulders. Typically the rock face can be used to stabilize the cheerleader and his/her handler. Once the cheerleader is within reach of the bolt, the quickdraw can be quickly deployed, and the cheerleader can hand-over-hand off of the handler's shoulders by using the climbing rope.

Improvised stick clip. For the sake of shoulders and sanity, many climbers prefer to improvise a stick clip. A long branch, limb, or stick should be scrounged from the nearby forest. Be conscientious about LNT principles in the search. It would be inappropriate to sever a living tree or limb, and it also would be inconsiderate to trample and deforest sensitive terrain in search of a stick. If a stick is not conveniently found, perhaps a different climb is more appropriate. The stick must be long enough to reach all the way to the first bolt, light enough to be held aloft, and strong enough to push a carabiner onto a bolt without flexing or breaking. Next, the bolt-clipping carabiner on a quickdraw should be taped to the end of the stick and a tiny twig can be used to hold the gate open while the stick reaches up to the first bolt. Meanwhile the climbing rope should be clipped into the rope-clipping carabiner on the same quickdraw. With the improvised stick clip configured thusly, the rope and quickdraw can be lifted up and connected to the first bolt. Be careful not to back clip. Lastly, a swift yank on the stick will rip the tape off the quickdraw, leaving the quickdraw and the rope ready for use. Pick up the tape! LNT—we see tape from stick clips left behind regularly at our local sport climbing venues!

Manufactured stick clip. Of course, a manufactured stick clip will save the climbing team a lot of time, tape, twigs, and energy, and this item is quickly becoming a signature tool of sport climbing. A manufactured stick clip usually has an extendable pole that is rigid, is lightweight, and collapses for easy transport. The clip has a clamp to hold the bolt-clipping carabiner, and some mechanism to hold the gate open while the climber reaches toward the first bolt. Some even have the capacity to clip the rope into fixed quickdraws.

Other methods. There are opportune techniques for a subsequent leader if a toprope is already hanging after an initial lead. While the leader lowers, he/she can unclip the second and third quickdraws as he/she low-ers. As a result, when the next leader is preparing to lead and pulls the rope, it will fall to the ground with the first quickdraw still clipped. Or, if none of the quick-draws is clipped but a toprope is in place, the lowering toproper can swing over and clip the belay strand into the first bolt. When the rope is pulled for the lead, the first bolt will already be clipped. Or, finally, a stick clip can be used to reach up above the first quickdraw and drag the rope down from above that point. As a result, when the rope is pulled from the rest of the quickdraws, the first bolt will already be clipped.

Shenanigans for Clipping a Fixed Draw

When fixed draws are already hanging on a sport climb, the most lauded technique involves lassoing the first bolt with a precisely swatted loop of rope. This tech-nique can be mastered only through unspeakable hours of practice, like any other parlor trick. But how impres-sive would it be to stride among the slip clippers and cheerleaders and, with John Wayne swagger, lasso the first bolt on the first try? It's good to have goals, right?

More practically, the slip clip is tried and true. A pair of unraveling rabbit ears can be tied on the stick clip so that when the stick clip is hoisted up to the first bolt, one rabbit ear can be looped around the carabiner while its counterpart secures the rope to the stick clip. With a quick slip of the noose, the rabbit ear collapses, the stick is removed, and the first quickdraw remains clipped.

Lastly, the same cheerleader technique can be used to clip a fixed draw, but in this case, the quickdraw is

Shenanigans 101: The stick clip slip clip in action on a fixed quickdraw!

already hanging on the pitch. The cheerleader will want to tie in, mount his/her handler's shoulders, clip the bolt, and then hand-over-hand back to the ground.

Shenanigans for Cleaning while Being Lowered

Frustratingly, the fall line for many sport climbing anchors is nowhere near the quickdraws that hang on the pitch, because the climb is overhanging. So cleaning the quickdraws usually involves covering a greater and greater distance between the landing zone and the bolts one is attempting to clean. One of the less frustrating solutions to this problem is for the leader to build a more compelling anchor, have another climber toprope up to the anchor, and clean the quickdraws along the way, eventually cleaning the anchor as well. However, it is not unheard of in combinations of sport climbers that one climber can lead climbs the other climber is not even able to toprope. That pairing of climbers would preclude the easier solution. Or both climbers may be equally interested in vying for the lead, which leaves cleaning the draws while lowering to someone else. Both may want to attach quickdraws on the lead, which would require cleaning after each lead.

Tramming is the preferred technique to recover those quickdraws. As the leader lowers, a quickdraw is clipped from the cleaner's belay loop to the strand of the rope that is running through all the quickdraws. This directional connection keeps the leader from swinging all the way back to the fall line beneath the anchor. As the cleaner approaches each quickdraw, he/she can hand–over–hand the belay strand of the system to get within reach of the quickdraw. But here is where the real shenanigans begin. If the cleaner is pulling on the belay strand or the direct quickdraw is pulling that line taut, it is difficult to remove the quickdraw from the bolt, because it is under tension. The dedicated cleaner should proceed to try one of three maneuvers until the quickdraw can be recovered.

First, the cleaner can grasp the quickdraw firmly and use that counterpoint to remove the belay strand of the rope from the quickdraw first. Then, with a bit of reach, the quickdraw can be removed from the bolt.

Second, the cleaner may be able to clip another directional quickdraw to the belay loop, swing toward the quickdraw he/she wishes to remove, and attach that second quickdraw to the lower side of the quickdraw slated for removal. At that point the cleaner will be attached to the belay strand by directional quickdraws above and below the targeted quickdraw. Shackled to the directional, the cleaner might find the quickdraws easier to reach and then remove. Or unclipping the top quickdraw might create the leverage the cleaner needs.

Tramming.

Lastly, the cleaner may resort to getting back on the holds of the climb, requesting just enough slack from the belayer to de-tension the system. The moment is tenuous and strenuous at this point, so the cleaner should unclip the quickdraw he/she wishes to remove from the bolt first, in this case. If the cleaner flies off the holds immediately thereafter, at least the quickdraw in question is free.

It should be noted that as the distance between the fall line and the anchor increases, the direction of pull or loading changes and forces increase. Because the overhang is so long, each bolt will be harder and harder to clean, requiring more and more shenanigans. Furthermore, the mechanical advantage created by the directional quickdraw also will increase as the cleaner approaches the last quickdraws. As a result, the belayer will need to be prepared to deal with these wrenching forces. Eventually, the cleaner will arrive at the last quickdraw. Imagine what would happen if the cleaner removed the last quickdraw without removing the directional quickdraw from his/her belay loop. It could be disastrous, depending on the climb. At worst, the cleaner would rapidly swing back to the fall line, dragging the belayer with him/her. It's an unwinnable tug-of-war that only a ground anchor could ameliorate. Better to remove that directional tramming quickdraw and hang on to rope or rock before cleaning the last bolt and get ready to swing back to the anchor's fall line.

Shenanigans for Reascending to a High Point after Falling

After a lead fall, the leader usually will want to climb back up to his/her high point. Batmanning up by

Batmanning and boinking.

pulling on the belay strand is one method, but there are occasions when the climb is so steep that the suspended climber cannot reach the belay strand. On these occasions it might be advisable to lower, rest, and give the lead another attempt. But many leaders will wish to continue to push their high point up the climb, in which case it's time to boink.

Boinking can be strenuous, but with enough dedication and an attentive belayer, it is effective. Remember, the point of boinking is to access the belay strand of the rope. Usually a couple of boinks will get the leader high enough to stretch out, grab the belay strand, and resume batmanning up the belay strand. To boink, the belay should suspend his/her body weight a few feet above the ground; an ABD is almost mandatory for these kinds of shenanigans. With the belayer slightly suspended, the leader must communicate with the belayer, "Ready?" The belayer should confirm, "Ready." Then the leader reaches overhead, grabs the climbing rope, and does a quick pull-up. It has to be quick, and the leader must have enough strength and grip to actually fling his/her body mass off of the belayer's counterweight. When the leader does so, the suspended belayer will drop a short distance, and that amount of rope can be drawn into the ABD as the belayer sets up for another boink. The process is exhausting for climber and belayer alike. Sport climbers learn to do what they have to.

Shenanigans for Hangdogging

Projecting

Since sport climbing invites a climber to the very limit of what is physically possible, many climbers learn that solving a climb is a bolt-by-bolt, sometimes inch-by-inch, endeavor. So, there are a variety of hangdogging shenanigans that can be deployed just to get through a particular move. This term in the early days of sport climbing was a derogatory one, as you were hanging and dogging it by resting. The ethic in these days was that a fall should be followed by a lower off (not a hang) and a reattempt at the lead.

Points of aid are often resorted to. Grabbing the textile of a quickdraw is sometimes just the little extra help a leader needs to get the rope clipped, to reach a better hold, or to completely bypass an intractable sequence. When resorting to this tactic, leaders should take heed to grab only the textile. Grabbing the carabiners can have unintended collateral consequences. The rope or the bolt could be inadvertently unclipped. The open carabiner could skewer the palm, clothing, or hair.

Additionally, many desperate leaders resorting to a point of aid have learned to connect a foot loop to the quickdraw to stand in. Sometimes a foothold in this loop is all the extra help a climber needs to access higher holds or another bolt.

The most "shameful" and risky hangdogging shenanigan involves trailing up a second rope. If there is a second rope trailed from the leader, there is a mechanism to ferry items up to the leader, like a stick clip. If the leader clips in to a bolt directly and ferries up a stick clip, the next bolt on the climb can be stick clipped and rope slack can be given from this position. The riskiness of this maneuver cannot be overstated, however. The leader is potentially setting him/herself up for a massive lead fall if their direct connection to the bolt is compromised during the stick-clipping procedure from all the rope slack. So, this technique should only even be considered when the leader is high enough to avert ground or ledge fall. Not to mention, all bystanders and the belayer must now be wary of a stick clip–wielding leader high off the ground.

Although this technique is an option, we divulge it with the sternest disclosure. This technique is risky, and it is not advisable. If deployed, it had better be worth it.

Retreating

At some point the leader may have had enough and will look to return to earth. This retreat may merely be a chance to rest, regroup, and climb back to the high point of the last quickdraw to try again. If the retreat is going to be the end of attempts for the day, there is probably a desire to retrieve the quickdraws placed, unless of course there are fixed quickdraws on the climb. When fixed quickdraws are present, simply lower off, lick your wounds, and move on. If this is not the case, aiding up to the anchor with a method described above is an option. Once you are at an anchor, it can be used to lower off and clean your quickdraws via processes outlined in this text.

If aiding is not an option or desirable, a lower from the climb is required. The best practice of redundancy should be adhered to. This means using at least two bolts to lower off from. This lowering process can be complex and may require some gear to be left behind. The type of bolt becomes a factor. Some types of fixed protection—Wave Bolts, some eye bolts, and the Metolius Rap hanger—allow the rope to run directly through them, but many do not. Not only do you have to assess the feasibility of the bolt to allow rope lowering, but the process requires directly connecting to a single bolt and threading the rope, a complex and risky process that we do not advocate.

A better approach is to transfer the rope to a carabiner or rapid link, also known as a leaver biner. Some may desire the extra security of a locking carabiner, and many prefer the rapid link for its locking feature and lower cost. To transfer to a leaver biner, place it in the bolt underneath the quickdraw, grab the quickdraw at the textile and pull up to generate a little slack (be careful), and clip the rope into the leaver biner. Get tension from your belayer, remove the quickdraw, communi-

A rapid link used to facilitate a lowering retreat. Use one from a reputable manufacturer.

cate, and lower to the next bolt. Repeat this process at least one other time and continue lowering and cleaning. Remember to value redundancy and lower from at least two bolts. When in doubt leave your quickdraws and lower. Someone else may be able to retrieve them for you or if "lost" they are a small price to pay for your safety. They are easily replaceable—you are worth it!

Shenanigans for Working with Others: The Mr./Mrs. Clean

Use after leading when you are working with an inexperienced partner/second and you do not want to reclimb the route to clean. Make your partner clean!

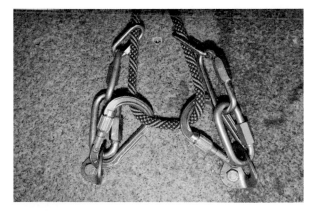

The Mr./Mrs. Clean.

Prerig an anchor with two locking carabiners or two locker draws and rig the climbing rope through the fixed anchor, so it does not load or wear. Your partner can become Mr./Mrs. Clean and simply remove these additions; the rope will load the fixed anchor and they can be lowered!

Emergency Preparedness

Awareness

Awareness of common risky, "spidey sense" moments like clipping, lowering, and rappelling is necessary. The procedures and best practices for these skills have been outlined in this text but are worthy of reemphasis here. Communicate a plan and follow best practices, and stay on a competent belay as often as possible. The renowned *Accidents in North American Mountaineering* is filled with tales of woe each year. Check out this text and learn from the mistakes of others.

Improvised Rescue Skills

This text cannot possibly cover the gamut of improvised rescue techniques in technical rock climbing.
The best way to learn a more comprehensive selection of these skills is to hire a professional climbing
instructor and work through a scenario-based cur-
riculum. But there are a couple techniques that will be
imminently useful to any climber, on any cliff, in any
scenario.

**Fixed line ascension with an ABD or Gri-
Gri, a friction hitch, and a double-length sling.**
Climbers should learn to climb a rope using some
basic ascension tools that they are already carrying.
A GriGri for example, due to the engagement of its
camming mechanism, can be used as a progress cap-
ture for rope ascension. A Prusik hitch and a double-
length sling can be used as an ascender and an etrier
(step). Together, the three tools will always allow res-
cuers to ascend a climbing rope. Why would this skill
be necessary? It may be necessary to assist a fallen or
stuck climber or deal with a stuck system.

To ascend with an ABD:

- Slide a friction hitch/sling combo up the rope and
  stand on it (the stand).

- Pull the rope through the ABD and sit on it (the
  sit).

- Repeat the stand and sit maneuvers for continued
  upward progress.

- Tie backup knots in the brake strand of the ABD
  (overhand on a bight) every 2 meters or so.

To descend with an ABD after ascending:

- Tie a new backup knot.

- Remove the friction hitch and sling and rappel with an ABD or a GriGri.

- Maintain a presence on the brake strand and untie the backup knots as you move down.

See *Climbing: Gym to Rock* for more details!

Hands-free at a belay. Climbers should learn to tie a mule knot when belaying with a tuber or plate. The mule knot allows the belayer to go hands-free and is backed up with an overhand. Going hands-free in and of itself may not solve many emergencies at the crag, but both hands might be needed to render first aid, make a cell phone call, or assist another rescuer.

The modern mule (left) and the classic mule (right) are both ways to go hands free with using a Manual Braking Device (MBD).

Conclusion

Hopefully there is a solid to-do list in an aspiring sport climber's mind. The foundations of protection and anchors and the host of technical skills required for maximizing your sport climbing experience and managing risk should be introduced in your mind. Taking personal responsibility, practicing and acquiring new skills and experiences within an appropriate progression, and being prepared to deal with all the realities of sport climbing will start your journey to effective sport climbing. Every chapter of this book outlines a part of your journey. The savvy sport climber tips, transition skills, and action steps should help guide you. The following steps outline a basic plan to take your skills from toproping to sport climbing.

Step 1: Take personal responsibility for what you know and what you don't know yet. Honestly self-assess your skills.

Step 2: Ensure your toproping skills are sharp and mastered; practice until you own them. (See *Climbing: Gym to Rock*, *Climbing: Knots*, and *Climbing: Protection*.) You can move with ease around a toproping crag, maximizing your day and managing risk and not need a more experienced person around.

Step 3: Learn to sport lead in a climbing gym. Work with a mentor or professional. Focus on lead belaying (MBD and ABD) and rope management and utilization throughout a sport lead climb. Many of the skills introduced in this text can be practiced at your local gym!

Step 4: Learn and grow. Perform another self-assessment. Go sport climbing outside with an experienced sport climbing leader. Second and support that leader all day: Be a belayer, observe the leader's skills in action, and practice the skills identified

Practice! Climbers simulate leading and lead belaying. This mock exercise occurs under the protection of a toprope and a separate belay.

in your self-assessment with low-consequence or simulated methods (like mock-belaying/leading). Get feedback and repeat.

Step 5: Engage with a professional. Hire an AMGA-certified climbing instructor or guide. See a high standard of climbing technical skills in action. Practice your skills under the watchful eye of an experienced and professional instructor. Get feedback as you learn to lead sport climbs.

Step 6: Research, pack, and go. Perform another self-assessment. Do your homework. Get the gear you need. Learn all about the crags you want to visit, the routes you want to do. Get psyched and prepared for your next outing.

Step 7: Go sport climbing with people of equal experience. Follow best practices as outlined in this text. Repeat.

Step 8: Go sport climbing with people of lesser experience. Perform yet another self-assessment. Are your skill sets honed and mastered to the point where it is sensible that you're the most experienced climber in your group? Repeat.

Step 9: Become an experienced, knowledgeable, and well-traveled climber. Build your climbing résumé. Go on a road trip—live the dream!

Have fun out there, and be careful.

An engaged sport climber in action!

About the Authors

Nate Fitch is a faculty member in the renowned Outdoor Education Department at the University of New Hampshire specializing in climbing courses/programing and is the director of the Gass Climbing Center. He is an AMGA–certified single-pitch instructor and apprentice rock guide who is also active in providing AMGA instructor programs as a climbing wall instructor and a single-pitch instructor assistant. He has climbed and instructed climbing all over the United States and abroad. Nate is the owner of Pawtuckaway Climbing School and Mountain Guides. He lives with his wife and two kids in Durham, New Hampshire.

Ron Funderburke is an AMGA-certified rock guide. He is the AMGA SPI Discipline Coordinator, the education manager at the American Alpine Club, and a senior climbing specialist with the North Carolina Outward Bound School. Ron lives in Golden, Colorado with his wife and sons.